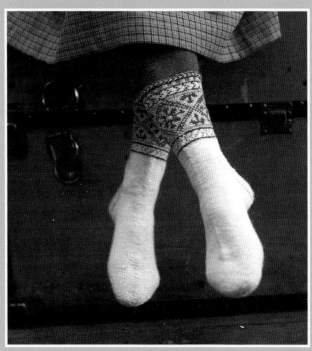

Favorite Socks

25 Timeless Designs *from* INTERWEAVE

Ann Budd and Anne Merrow, EDITORS

INTERWEAVE PRESS.

Photography: Chris Hartlove, unless otherwise noted
Cover photo: Joe Coca
Text, illustrations, photography ©2006, Interweave Press LLC

 INTERWEAVE PRESS
www.interweave.com

201 East Fourth Street
Loveland, CO 80537

Printed in China by Asia Pacific Offset

Library of Congress Cataloging-in-Publication Data
Favorite socks : 25 timeless designs from Interweave / Ann Budd, Anne Merrow, editors.
   p. cm.
 Includes index.
 ISBN-13: 978-1-59668-032-6 (pbk.)
 1. Knitting--Patterns. 2. Socks. I. Budd, Ann, 1956- II. Merrow, Anne, 1977-
TT825.F39 2007
746.43'20432--dc22
                    2006023490

10 9 8 7 6 5 4 3 2 1

CONTENTS

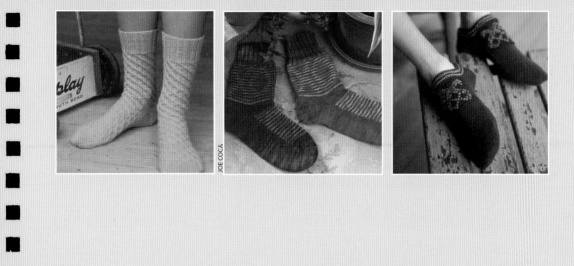

JOE COCA

INTRODUCTION

In its first decade of publication, *Interweave Knits* has published dozens of sock designs. The second issue, published in the Spring of 1997, included our first sock pattern by sock designer extraordinaire Nancy Bush, a lovely pair of Estonian-inspired lace socks called Meida's Socks. For the first few years, socks appeared sporadically, but soon we realized that these were among the most popular projects each issue. And why wouldn't they be? Besides the practical benefits—socks are portable, useful, relatively quick, and almost universally wearable—there's both luxurious pleasure and primal comfort in covering your feet (or those of someone you really like) with thousands of knitted stitches.

Interweave Knits and other Interweave publications have offered patterns for knitted socks plain and fancy, eminently practical and arguably decadent, traditional and modern. These socks are made top-down, bottom-up, side-to-side, and in every stitch pattern imaginable. Over the years, many of these patterns have become unavailable as the original issues went out-of-print, although the socks themselves are timeless.

For this collection, we've chosen seventeen of our favorite designs, some of which were published before many current readers first picked up needles and yarn. You'll find socks from old issues, like Meida's Socks, and patterns from more recent issues. Even the most dedicated readers of *Knits* probably haven't seen the Anniversary Socks, also by Nancy Bush, which appeared in the tenth anniversary issue of *Knits'* sister publication *PieceWork*, or the clever Two-Yarn Resoleable Socks from another sister publication, *Spin•Off.* And because we can't resist an opportunity to create some new classics, we've included six entirely new sock patterns, so even if you have every issue of *Knits* since 1996, you're sure to find new inspiration.

This blend of new projects and old favorites will keep your needles flying and your feet warm. Look through the pages of this book and share our wonder at the ingenuity of sock knitters everywhere.

from the Winter 2004 issue of *Interweave Knits*

Retro Rib Socks

Evelyn A. Clark

Simple knit and purl stitches are bordered by a neat twisted rib in these easy unisex socks with retro appeal. The smart stitch pattern, a combination of knits, purls, and knit-through-the-back-loops, is manageable for a beginning sock knitter. Comfortable and classic, they'll be instant favorites.

FINISHED SIZE
About 7 (7¾)" (18 [19.5] cm) foot circumference and 9¼ (10)" (23.5 [25.5] cm) foot length. To fit a woman (man). *Note:* The ribbed pattern is very elastic— both sizes have the same number of stitches in the leg.

YARN
Fingering-weight yarn (CYCA #1 Super Fine).
Shown here: Kroy Socks (75% wool, 25% nylon; 203 yd [187 m]/ 50 g): 2 (3) balls. Shown in #54105 regatta blue and #54013 hickory.

NEEDLES
Size 2 (2.75 mm): set of 5 double-pointed (dpn). Adjust needle size if necessary to obtain the correct gauge.

NOTIONS
Markers (m); tapestry needle.

GAUGE
16 stitches and 22 rounds = 2" (10 cm) in stockinette stitch worked in the round.

STITCH GUIDE
Instep Pattern (multiple of 8 sts + 2)
Rnd 1: *P2, k1 through back loop (k1tbl), p4, k1tbl; rep from *, end p2.
Rnd 2: *P2, k1, p4, k1; rep from *, end p2.
Rnd 3: *P2, k1tbl, p1, k2, p1, k1tbl; rep from *, end p2.
Rnd 4: *P2, k1, p1, k2, p1, k1; rep from *, end p2.
Repeat Rnds 1–4 for pattern.

Leg

Loosely CO 64 sts. Arrange sts evenly on 4 dpn, place marker (pm), and join for working in the rnd, being careful not to twist sts.

Ribbing

Rnd 1: Purl.

Rnd 2: *P2, k1 through back loop (k1tbl), p1, k2, p1, k1tbl; rep from *.

Rnd 3: *P2, k1, p1, k2, p1, k1; rep from *.

Work Rnds 2 and 3 a total of 6 times— 15 rnds total. Cont as foll:

Rnd 1: *P2, k1tbl, p4, k1tbl; rep from *.

Rnd 2: *P2, k1, p4, k1; rep from *.

Rnd 3: *P2, k1tbl, p1, k2, p1, k1tbl; rep from *.

Rnd 4: *P2, k1, p1, k2, p1, k1; rep from *.

Rep these 4 rnds 17 (19) times total, ending with Rnd 4—piece measures about 8 (8½)" (20.5 [21.5] cm) from CO.

Heel

Heel Flap

K15, turn work around, sl 1 pwise with yarn in front (wyf), p29—30 heel sts centered at back of leg; rem 34 sts will be worked later for instep. Work 30 heel sts back and forth in rows as foll:

Row 1: (RS) *Sl 1 pwise with yarn in back (wyb), k1; rep from *.

Row 2: (WS) Sl 1 pwise wyf, p29.

Rep these 2 rows 15 (17) times total, then work Row 1 once more—15 (17) chain sts along each selvedge edge; heel flap measures about 2½ (2¾)" (6.5 [7] cm) long.

Turn Heel

Work short-rows to shape heel as foll:

Row 1: (WS) Sl 1 pwise wyf, p16, p2tog, p1, turn work.

Row 2: (RS) Sl 1 pwise wyb, k5, ssk, k1, turn.

Row 3: Sl 1 pwise wyf, p6, p2tog, p1, turn.

Cont in this manner, working 1 more st before dec each row until all heel sts have been worked—18 heel sts rem.

Shape Gussets

Pick up sts along selvedge edges of heel flap and rejoin for working in the rnd as foll:

Rnd 1: With Needle 1 (needle holding heel sts), pick up and knit 17 (19) sts along edge of heel flap; with Needle 2 and Needle 3, work Rnd 1 of instep patt (see Stitch Guide) across 34 instep sts; with Needle 4, pick up and knit 17 (19) sts along other edge of heel flap, then knit first 9 heel sts from Needle 1 again— 86 (90) sts total; 26 (28) sts each on Needle 1 and Needle 4; 16 sts on Needle 2; 18 sts on Needle 3. Rnd begins at center of heel.

Rnd 2: On Needle 1, k9, k17 (19) through back loops; on Needle 2 and Needle 3, cont in instep patt as established; on Needle 4, k17 (19) through back loops, k9.

Rnd 3: On Needle 1, knit to last 2 sts, k2tog; on Needle 2 and Needle 3, cont in instep patt as established; on Needle 4, ssk, knit to end—2 sts dec'd.

Rnd 4: On Needle 1, knit; on Needle 2 and Needle 3, cont in instep patt; on Needle 4, knit.

Rep Rnds 3 and 4 until 64 (68) sts rem—15 (17) sts each on Needle 1 and Needle 4; 16 sts on Needle 2; 18 sts on Needle 3.

Foot

Cont as established (work instep patt on Needle 2 and Needle 3; work St st on Needle 1 and Needle 4) until piece measures about 7½ (8)" (19 [20.5] cm) from back of heel, or about 1¾ (2)" (4.5 [5] cm) less than desired total foot length.

Toe

Knit all sts on next rnd, and *at the same time* redistribute sts so that there are 16 (17) sts on each needle, with the instep sts evenly divided between Needle 2 and Needle 3 and the sole sts evenly divided between Needle 1 and Needle 4.

Rnd 1: On Needle 1, knit to last 3 sts, k2tog, k1; on Needle 2, k1, ssk, knit to end of needle; on Needle 3, knit to last 3 sts, k2tog, k1; on Needle 4, k1, ssk, knit to end of needle—4 sts dec'd.

Rnd 2: Knit.

Rep Rnds 1 and 2 until 32 sts rem. Rep Rnd 1 *every* rnd until 16 sts rem. With Needle 4, knit 4 sts on Needle 1; sl 4 sts from Needle 3 onto Needle 2—8 sts each on 2 needles.

Finishing

Cut yarn, leaving a 12" (30.5 cm) tail. Thread tail on a tapestry needle and use the Kitchener st (see Glossary, page 123) to graft sts tog. Weave in loose ends. Block lightly.

ELEGANT RIBBED STOCKINGS

Ann Budd

These elegant stockings taper from knee to ankle by decreasing the needle size instead of changing the stitch count. The simple but distinctive cable pattern, reminiscent of antique stonework, makes these socks fit closely but comfortably. A row of subtle eyelets beneath the ribbed cuff can accommodate a pretty ribbon accent.

FINISHED SIZE
About 6¾ (8)" (17 [20.5] cm) foot circumference and 9 (10)" (23 [25.5] cm) foot length. To fit a child (woman). *Note:* To make the socks larger or smaller, use needles one or two sizes larger or smaller and lengthen or shorten the foot as necessary.

YARN
Sportweight yarn (CYCA #2 Fine).
Shown here: Dale of Norway Heilo (100% wool; 109 yd [100 m]/50 g): #9834 antique gold, 4 balls.

NEEDLES
Ribbing and middle leg—size 6 (4 mm): set of 4 double-pointed (dpn). Upper leg—size 7 (4.5 mm): set of 4 dpn. Lower leg and foot—size 5 (3.75 mm): set of 4 dpn. Adjust needle sizes if necessary to obtain correct gauge.

NOTIONS
Cable needle (cn); marker (m); tapestry needle; about 2 yd (2 meter) 1" (2.5 cm) Hanah Silk Hand Dyed Ribbon in colorway Monet (optional).

GAUGE
12 stitches and 17 rounds = 2" (5 cm) in stockinette stitch worked in the round on size 5 (3.75 mm) needles.

Leg

With size 6 (4 mm) needles and using the old Norwegian method (see Glossary, page 121), loosely CO 48 (56) sts. Arrange sts on 3 dpn so that there are 16 (20) sts on Needle 1, 16 (20) sts on Needle 2, and 16 (16) sts on Needle 3. Place marker (pm) and join for working in the rnd, being careful not to twist sts. Work Rows 1–5 *only* of Elegant Ribbing chart 2 (3) times— 10 (15) rnds total. *Eyelet rnd:* (optional) *K1, yo, p2tog, k1; rep from * to end of rnd. Change to size 7 (4.5 mm) needles and work Rnds 5–14 of chart once, then work Rnds 1–14 of chart once more. Cont in patt, rep Rnds 1–14 of chart and *at the same time,* when piece measures 5 (6)" (12.5 [15] cm) from CO, change to size 6 (4 mm) needles, then when piece measures 9 (10)" (23 [25.5] cm) from CO, change to size 5 (3.75 mm) needles. Cont even in patt until leg measures about 12 (13½)" (30.5 [34.5] cm) from CO or desired length to top of heel, ending with Rnd 11 of chart.

Elegant Ribbing

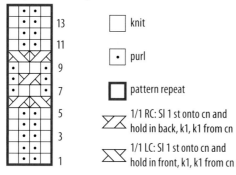

13

11

9

7

5

3

1

☐ knit

· purl

☐ pattern repeat

1/1 RC: Sl 1 st onto cn and hold in back, k1, k1 from cn

1/1 LC: Sl 1 st onto cn and hold in front, k1, k1 from cn

Heel

Heel Flap

K10 (14), turn work around so WS is facing, sl 1 pwise with yarn in front (wyf), p23 (27)— 24 (28) heel sts centered at back of leg (when viewed from RS, these sts beg and end with p1); rem 24 (28) sts will be worked later for instep. Work 24 (28) heel sts back and forth in rows as foll:

Row 1: (RS) Sl 1 kwise with yarn in back (wyb), *k1, sl 1 pwise wyb; rep from * to last st, k1.

Row 2: (WS) Sl 1 pwise with yarn in front (wyf), purl to end.

Rep Rows 1 and 2 until a total of 24 (28) rows have been worked—12 (14) chain sts along each selvedge edge.

Turn Heel

Work short-rows to shape heel as foll:

Row 1: (RS) K14 (16), ssk, k1, turn work.

Row 2: (WS) Sl 1 pwise wyf, p5, p2tog, p1, turn.

Row 3: Sl 1 kwise wyb, knit to 1 st before gap formed on previous row, ssk (1 st from each side of gap), k1, turn.

Row 4: Sl 1 pwise wyf, purl to 1 st before gap formed on previous row, p2tog (1 st from each side of gap), p1, turn.

Rep Rows 3 and 4 until all heel sts have been worked—14 (16) heel sts rem.

Shape Gussets

Pick up sts along selvedge edges of heel flap and rejoin for working in the rnd as foll:

Rnd 1: With Needle 1, k14 (16) heel sts then pick up and knit 13 (15) sts along edge of heel flap; with Needle 2, work across 24 (28) instep sts in rib patt as established; with Needle 3, pick up and knit 1 3 (15) sts along other edge of heel flap, then knit the first 7 (8) heel sts from Needle 1 again—64 (74) sts total; 20 (23) sts each on Needle 1 and Needle 3; 24 (28) instep sts on Needle 2. Rnd begins at center of heel.

Rnd 2: On Needle 1, knit to last 3 sts, k2tog, k1; on Needle 2, work in rib patt as established; on Needle 3, k1, ssk, knit to end—2 sts dec'd.

Rnd 3: Cont in patt as established (work sts on Needle 2 in patt from chart; work sts on Needle 1 and Needle 3 in St st).

Rep Rnds 2 and 3 until 48 (56) sts rem.

Foot

Cont even in patt as established until piece measures about 7 (8)" (18 [20.5] cm) from back of heel, or about 2" (5 cm) less than desired total foot length.

Toe

Work in St st as foll:

Rnd 1: On Needle 1, knit to last 3 sts, k2tog k1; on Needle 2, k1, ssk, knit to last 3 sts, k2tog, k1; on Needle 3, k1, ssk, knit to end—4 sts dec'd.

Rnd 2: Knit.

Rep Rnds 1 and 2 until 24 (28) sts rem. Rep Rnd 1 *every* rnd until 8 (12) sts rem. Knit the sts on Needle 1 onto the end of Needle 3— 4 (6) sts each on 2 needles.

JOE COCA

Finishing

Cut yarn, leaving a 12" (30.5 cm) tail. Thread tail on a tapestry needle and use the Kitchener st (see Glossary, page 123) to graft sts tog. Weave in loose ends. Block lightly. Beg and end at outside of leg, thread optional silk ribbon through eyelets at top of stocking. Tie ends into a bow.

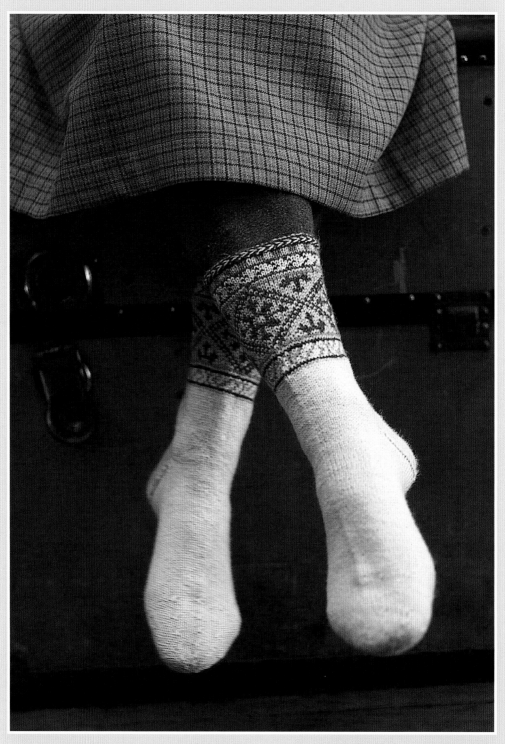

from the Spring 2001 issue of *Interweave Knits*

Ilga's Socks

Nancy Bush

Common Latvian mythological symbols inspired this design. *Laima*, signified by the arrowlike pattern beneath the braided top edge, is one of three main Latvian deities and the controller of destiny. *Zalktis*, the grass snake represented in the curling border at the bottom of the color-work band, is a good omen, guarding everything good and valuable and acting as an intermediary between earth and sky. *Mara*, seen here in the design between Laima and Zalktis, is a helper of God and protector of women. The socks are named for Ilga Madre, a talented Latvian knitter.

FINISHED SIZE
About 8" (20.5 cm) foot circumference and 9¼" (23.5 cm) foot length. To fit a woman. *Note:* To make the socks larger or smaller, use needles one or two sizes larger or smaller and lengthen or shorten the foot as necessary.

YARN
Fingering-weight yarn (CYCA #1 Super Fine).
Shown here: Vuorelman Satakieli (100% wool; 350 yd [320 m]/ 100 g): #003 natural (MC), #132 pale yellow (A), #184 sun yellow (B), #966 indigo (C), and #985 khaki green (D), 1 skein each.

NEEDLES
Cuff—size 1 (2.25 mm): set of 5 double-pointed (dpn). Leg and foot—size 0 (2 mm): set of 5 dpn. Adjust needle sizes if necessary to obtain the correct gauge.

NOTIONS
Marker (m); tapestry needle.

GAUGE
18 stitches and 24 rounds = 2" (5 cm) in stockinette stitch worked in the round on size 0 (2 mm) needles.

STITCH GUIDE
Latvian Braid
Rnd 1: *K1 with A, k1 with C; rep from *.
Rnd 2: *P1 with A, p1 with C, always bringing the new yarn *over* the one just used; rep from *.
Rnd 3: *P1 with A, p1 with C, always bringing the new yarn *under* the one just used; rep from *.

Leg

With A, C, size 1 (2.25 mm) needles, and using the long-tail method (see Glossary, page 120), holding A over the index finger and C over the thumb, CO 76 sts. Arrange sts evenly on 4 dpn (19 sts each needle), place marker (pm), and join for working in the rnd, being careful not to twist sts. Rnd begins at back of leg. Work Rnds 1–3 of Latvian braid (see Stitch Guide). Work Rnds 1–44 of Cuff chart, dec 4 sts evenly spaced on Rnd 13—72 sts rem; 18 sts each needle. Change to size 0 (2 mm) needles and MC only, and work even in St st until leg measures 7" (18 cm) or desired length to beg of heel, ending last rnd at end of Needle 3.

✓ natural (MC)	☐ pale yellow (A)
✗ indigo (C)	– khaki green (D)
▫ sun yellow (B)	▢ pattern repeat

Cuff

Heel

Heel Flap

Work heel flap back and forth in rows as foll:

Row 1: (RS) *Sl 1, k1; rep from * across 36 sts (all sts on Needle 4 and Needle 1)—36 heel sts; rem 36 sts will be worked later for instep.

Row 2: (WS) Sl 1 pwise with yarn in front (wyf), p35.

Row 3: Sl 1 kwise with yarn in back (wyb), *sl 1 kwise wyb, k1; rep from *, end last rep k2.

Row 4: Sl 1 pwise wyf, p35.

Rep Rows 1–4 until a total of 36 rows have been worked, ending with Row 4—18 chain sts along each selvedge edge.

Turn Heel

Work short-rows to shape heel as foll:

Row 1: K20, ssk, k1, turn work.

Row 2: Sl 1, p5, p2tog, p1, turn.

Row 3: Sl 1, knit to 1 st before gap formed on previous row, ssk (1 st each side of gap), k1, turn.

Row 4: Sl 1, purl to 1 st before gap formed on previous row, p2tog (1 st each side of gap), p1, turn.

Rep Rows 3 and 4 until all sts have been worked—20 heel sts rem.

Shape Gussets

Pick up sts along selvedge edges of heel flap and rejoin for working in the rnd as foll:

Rnd 1: With Needle 1, k20 heel sts then pick up and knit 18 sts along right edge of heel flap; with Needle 2, work first 18 instep sts; with Needle 3, work rem 18 instep sts; with Needle 4, pick up and knit 18 sts along left edge of heel flap, then knit first 10 heel sts from Needle 1 again—92 sts total; 28 sts on Needle 1; 18 sts each on Needle 2 and Needle 3; 28 sts on Needle 4. Rnd begins at center of heel.

Rnd 2: On Needle 1, work to last 3 sts, k2tog, k1; on Needle 2 and Needle 3, work instep sts as established; on Needle 4, k1, ssk, work to end—2 sts dec'd.

Rnd 3: Work even in patt.

Rep Rnds 2 and 3 until 72 sts rem—18 sts each needle.

Foot

Work even until piece measures about 7¼" (18.5 cm) from back of heel or about 2½" (6.5 cm) less than desired total foot length.

Toe

Dec Rnd 1: *K6, k2tog; rep from *—63 sts rem.

Work 6 rnds even.

Dec Rnd 2: *K5, k2tog; rep from *—54 sts rem.

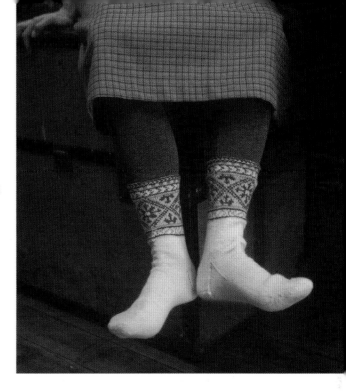

Work 5 rnds even.

Dec Rnd 3: *K4, k2tog; rep from *—45 sts rem.

Work 4 rnds even.

Dec Rnd 4: *K3, k2tog; rep from *—36 sts rem.

Work 3 rnds even.

Dec Rnd 5: *K2, k2tog; rep from *—27 sts rem.

Work 2 rnds even.

Dec Rnd 6: *K1, k2tog; rep from *—18 sts rem.

Work 1 rnd even.

Dec Rnd 7: *K2tog; rep from *—9 sts rem.

Finishing

Cut yarn, leaving a 12" (30.5 cm) tail. Thread tail through rem sts, pull snug to tighten, and fasten off. Weave in loose ends. Block lightly.

from the Winter 2003 issue of *Interweave Knits*

Uptown Boot Socks

Jennifer L. Appleby

A versatile designer, Jennifer Appleby blends style with practicality to create knitwear with rustic elegance. These socks are a perfect example: a fluid, allover cable pattern in a sock-weight yarn provides an upscale touch, while the thicker fabric and "slouch" design make for sturdy, comfortable socks suitable for casual or dressy use. A modern classic.

Finished Size

About 7 (8¼, 9¾)" (18 [21, 25] cm) foot circumference and 8¼ (10, 11¼)" (21 [25.5, 28.5] cm) foot length. To fit a child (woman, man).

Yarn

Fingering-weight yarn (CYCA #1 Super Fine).
Shown here: Schoeller-Stahl Zimba Top (80% wool, 20% nylon; 164 yd [150 m]/50 g): #105 celery, 3 (3, 4) balls.

Needles

Size 2 (2.75 mm): set of 4 double-pointed (dpn). Adjust needle size if necessary to obtain the correct gauge.

Notions

Cable needle (cn); tapestry needle.

Gauge

16½ stitches and 20 rounds = 2" (5 cm) in cable pattern worked in the round.

Stitch Guide

Cable Pattern (multiple of 8 sts)
Rnds 1 and 2: Knit.
Rnd 3: *Sl 2 sts onto cn and hold in front, k2, k2 from cn, k4; rep from *.
Rnds 4–6: Knit.
Rnd 7: *K4, sl 2 sts onto cn and hold in front, k2, k2 from cn; rep from *.
Rnd 8: Knit.
Repeat Rnds 1–8 for pattern.

Leg

Loosely CO 64 (72, 80) sts. Arrange sts on 3 dpn as foll: 20 (24, 28) sts each on Needle 1 and Needle 3; 24 sts on Needle 2. Join for working in the rnd, being careful not to twist sts. *K2, p2; rep from * until piece measures 2½" (6.5 cm) from beg. Work Rows 1–8 of cable patt (see Stitch Guide) until piece measures 8 (8, 10)" (20.5 [20.5, 25.5] cm) from CO.

Heel

Heel Flap

Place first 16 sts of Needle 1 and last 16 sts of Needle 3 onto one needle—32 sts total for heel; rem 32 (40, 48) sts will be worked later for instep. Cut yarn. With WS facing, rejoin yarn to 32 heel sts and purl these sts, dec 4 (4, 0) sts evenly spaced as you go— 28 (28, 32) heel sts rem.

Row 1: (RS) *Sl 1 pwise with yarn in back (wyb), k1; rep from *.

Row 2: (WS) Sl 1 pwise with yarn in front (wyf), purl to end.

Rep Rows 1 and 2 until flap measures 2 (2¼, 2½)" (5 [5.5, 6.5] cm), ending with a WS row.

Turn Heel

Sl 1 pwise wyb, knit to end, dec 4 (0, 0) sts evenly spaced as you go—24 (28, 32) heel sts rem. Work short-rows to shape heel as foll:

Row 1: (WS) Sl 1 pwise wyf, p13 (17, 19), p2tog, p1, turn work.

Row 2: (RS) Sl 1 pwise wyb, k5 (9, 9), sl 1, k1, psso, k1, turn.

Row 3: Sl 1 pwise wyf, p6 (10, 10), p2tog, p1, turn.

Cont in this manner, working 1 more st before dec for 5 (5, 7) more rows—8 (8, 10) short-rows total. *Next row:* (WS) Sl 1, p12 (16, 18), p2tog. *Next row:* Sl 1, k12 (16, 18), sl 1, k1, psso—14 (18, 20) sts rem.

Shape Gussets

Pick up sts along selvedge edges of heel flap and rejoin for working in the rnd as foll:

Rnd 1: Place 32 (40, 48) held instep sts onto 1 dpn. With RS facing and Needle 1 (needle holding heel sts), pick up and knit 14 (15, 16) sts along edge of heel flap; with Needle 2, work cable patt as established across 32 (40, 48) instep sts; with Needle 3, pick up and knit 14 (15, 16) sts along other edge of heel flap, then knit first 7 (9, 10) heel st from Needle 1 again—74 (88, 100) sts total. Place rem 7 (9, 10) heel sts onto Needle 1—21 (24, 26) sts each on Needle 1 and Needle 3; 32 (40, 48) sts on Needle 2. Rnd begins at center of heel.

Rnd 2: On Needle 1, knit to last 3 sts, k2tog, k1; on Needle 2, work cable patt as established; on Needle 3, ssk, knit to end—2 sts dec'd.

Rnd 3: Work even as established.

Rep Rnds 2 and 3 until 58 (68, 80) sts rem—13 (14, 16) sts each on Needle 1 and Needle 3; 32 (40, 48) sts on Needle 2.

Foot

Cont even as established until piece measures about 5 (6, 6¾)" (12.5 [15, 17] cm) from beg of gusset.

Toe

Size small only:

Rnd 1: On Needle 1, knit to last 3 sts, k2tog, k1; on Needle 2, k1, ssk, k8, ssk, k6, k2tog, k8, k2tog, k1; on Needle 3, k1, ssk, knit to end—12 sts each on Needle 1 and Needle 3; 28 sts on Needle 2.

Rnds 2 and 4: Knit.

Rnd 3: On Needle 1, knit to last 3 sts, k2tog, k1; on Needle 2, k1, ssk, k2, ssk, k5, ssk, k2tog, k5, k2tog, k2, k2tog, k1; on Needle 3, k1, ssk, knit to end—11 sts each on Needle 1 and Needle 3; 22 sts on Needle 2.

Sizes medium (large):

Rnd 1: On Needle 1, knit; on Needle 2, k1, ssk, k5, ssk, k8 (k5, ssk, k5), ssk, k2tog, k8 (k5, k2tog, k5), k2tog, k5, k2tog, k1; on Needle 3, knit—14 (16) sts each on Needle 1 and Needle 3; 34 (40) sts on Needle 2.

Rnds 2 and 4: Knit.

Rnd 3: On Needle 1, knit; on Needle 2, k1, ssk, k3, ssk, k6 (4), ssk, k2 (k3, ssk, k2), k2tog, k6 (k3, k2tog, k4), k2tog, k3, k2tog, k1; on Needle 3, knit—14 (16) sts each on Needle 1 and Needle 3; 28 (32) sts on Needle 2.

All sizes:

Rnd 5: On Needle 1, knit to last 3 sts, k2tog, k1; on Needle 2, k1, ssk, knit to last 3 sts, k2tog, k1; on Needle 3, k1, ssk, knit to end—40 (52, 60) sts rem; 10 (13, 15) sts each on Needle 1 and Needle 2; 20 (26, 30) sts on Needle 2.

Rnd 6: Knit.

Rep Rnds 5 and 6 until 24 (24, 28) sts rem.

Size small only:

On Needle 1, k3, k2tog, k1; on Needle 2, k1, ssk, k2, k2tog, k2, k2tog, k1; on Needle 3, k1, ssk, k2, k2tog (last st of Needle 3 and first st of Needle 1)—18 sts rem.

All sizes:

With Needle 3, knit all sts of Needle 1— 9 (12, 14) sts each on 2 needles.

Finishing

Cut yarn, leaving a 12" (30.5 cm) tail. Thread tail on a tapestry needle and use the Kitchener st (see Glossary, page 123) to graft sts tog. Weave in loose ends. Block lightly.

from the Fall 2000 issue of *Interweave Knits*

PRISCILLA'S DREAM SOCKS

Priscilla Gibson-Roberts

While studying handknitted socks from around the world, Priscilla Gibson-Roberts always hoped to find the perfect structure: a well-fitting sock that is durable, flexible in design, and easy to knit and repair. To her surprise, she found the key in a pair of machine-made socks. The store-bought socks fit perfectly, and upon closer examination Priscilla found that her dream sock included short-rows at both heel and toe. Although short-row heels are a handknitting mainstay, short-row toes are uncommon outside machine knitting.

FINISHED SIZE
About 8" (20.5 cm) foot circumference and 9" (23 cm) foot length. To fit a woman.

YARN
Sportweight yarn (CYCA #2 Fine).
Shown here: Dale of Norway Tiur (60% mohair, 40% wool; 126 yd [115 m]/50 g): Solid Socks: #4136 red, 3 skeins. Striped Socks: #7053 teal, 2 skeins; #5111 silver, 1 skein.

NEEDLES
Upper leg—size 3 (3.25 mm): set of 5 double-pointed (dpn). Lower leg and foot—size 2 (2.75 mm): set of 5 dpn. Adjust needle sizes if necessary to obtain the correct gauge.

NOTIONS
Tapestry needle.

GAUGE
16 stitches and 20 rows = 2" (5 cm) in stockinette stitch worked in the round on size 2 (2.75 mm) needles.

STITCH GUIDE
sssp
Slip 3 sts individually kwise, place these 3 sts back onto left needle, take right needle behind these 3 sts and purl them together through their back loops.

Instructions are given below for the socks shown in the photograph. To knit these socks in a different size or gauge, refer to the chart on page 29.

Plain Socks

Leg

With size 3 (3.25 mm) needles and using the old Norwegian method (see Glossary, page 121), CO 64 sts. Arrange sts evenly on 4 dpn so that there are 16 sts on each needle. Join for working in the rnd, being careful not to twist sts. Rnd begins at the inside of the leg. *Set up ribbing:* K1, *p2, k2; rep from *, end k1. Cont as established, work k2, p2 ribbing until piece measures about 3½" (9 cm) from CO. Change to size 2 (2.75 mm) needles and cont as established until piece measures 7" (18 cm) from CO. Change to St st and work 12 rnds, ending last rnd at end of Needle 4.

Heel

The heel is worked back and forth in short-rows on the 32 sts on Needle 1 and Needle 2 for left sock (Needle 3 and Needle 4 for right sock).

Heel Back

Row 1: (RS) K31, turn work.

Row 2: Yo backwards (see box "Heel and Toe Construction" on page 27), p30 (do not work the last st), turn.

Row 3: Yo, knit to paired sts made by yo of previous row (the yo will form a loop out of the side of the adjacent st), leaving 3 sts on left needle (i.e., do not knit the pair), turn.

Row 4: Yo backwards, purl to paired sts made by the yo of the previous row, turn.

Rep these last 2 rows until there are 10 unpaired sts in the center of the heel and 12 sts total bet yarnovers (10 sts between the paired sts plus 1 st from the first paired st on each side), ending with a RS row, but do not turn. This becomes the first row of the heel base.

Heel Base

Row 1: K1 (the first st of the pair), correct the mount of the yo (sl the yo pwise, enter slipped yo with the left needle tip from front to back to correct the stitch mount, place it on left needle), k2tog (the yo with the first st of the next pair, leaving a yo as the first st on the left needle), turn.

Row 2: (WS) Yo backwards, purl to paired st made by yo of previous row, purl the first st of the pair, ssp (the yo with the first st of the next pair, leaving a yo as the first st on the left needle; see Glossary, page 122), turn.

Row 3: Yo, knit to the paired st made by yo of previous row, knit the first st of the pair (the next 2 loops will be yos), correct the mount of each of these yos, k3tog (2 yos with the first st of the next pair), turn.

Row 4: Yo backwards, purl to next yo, (the next 2 loops are yos), sssp (2 yos with the first st of the next pair; see Stitch Guide), turn.

Row 5: Yo, knit to next yo (the next 2 loops will be yos), correct the mount of each of these yos, k3tog (2 yos with the first st of the next pair), turn.

Rep the last 2 rows until all yos of the heel back have been consumed, ending with Row 4. The last turn will bring RS facing. Yo, knit to end of Needle 1—17 sts each on Needle 1 and Needle 2 (16 regular sts plus 1 yo). Knit to the yo at the end of Needle 2, place this yo onto Needle 3 (instep needle), k2tog (the yo plus first st of Needle 3), work to last st on Needle 4, place last st on Needle 4 onto Needle 1 and ssk (last st of Needle 4 plus yo at beg of Needle 1)— 64 sts rem. (*Note:* This final dec may appear to form a gap if the sts loosened while the heel was worked. To minimize the gap, work the dec and several more sts on this row onto Needle 4, then reposition the sts on the needles later, or close the gap by picking up 1 st in the gap onto the left needle, place the last st on Needle 4 onto Needle 1, and sssk.)

Foot

Cont even until piece measures 7" (18 cm) from back of heel.

Toe

Work toe exactly as the heel—work the sole half of the toe sts as for the heel back, then work the instep half of the toe sts as for the heel base. After making the last turn, the RS of the toe top will be facing. Join the toe sts to the top of the foot sts with a zigzag bind-off (a technique borrowed from historic Greek knitting): Align sts on 2 needles, 1 for the toe sts and 1 for the foot sts. Holding these 2 needles tog, p1 from back needle, k1 from front needle, pass first st over, *p1 from back needle, pass front st over, k1 from front needle, pass back st over; rep from * until 1 st rem on needle, working last st tog with its accompanying yo. Break yarn and draw tail through last st. (If you'd prefer an invisible join, work the top of the toe first, then the bottom, then use the Kitchener st [see Glossary, page 123] to graft the toe sts to the sole sts. This places the graft on the sole where tension irregularities will be less noticeable.)

Heel and Toe Construction

The heel and toe are constructed with short-rows that produce an hourglass shape. Each short-row begins with a yarnover that is instrumental in preventing gaps. When the knit side is facing, work the yarnover in the standard manner, bringing yarn forward under needle then over the top to the back. When the purl side is facing, bring yarn to the back under needle, then over the top to the front as illustrated below. This forms a "backward" yarnover—the leading side of the loop is on the back of the needle—but the distance traveled by the yarn will equal that of the standard yarnover on the knit side, an important distinction for truly even stitches. The stitch mount will be corrected later.

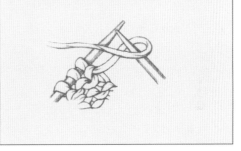

Striped Socks

Leg

With teal, CO 64 sts as for plain sock. Work leg as for plain version, alternating 4 rnds teal with 4 rnds silver 8 times total in k2, p2 rib, then change to St st and work 4 rnds teal, 4 rnds silver, 4 rnds teal, then 2 rnds silver.

Heel

The heel on one sock is worked on Needle 1 and Needle 2, with the first stitch in silver, changing to teal for the rest of the heel. When the last turn has been made, change to silver, decreasing with k2tog on the first side, ssk at the other. Complete 4-row stripe in silver. To center the joins on the opposite side for the second sock, work the heel on Needle 3 and Needle 4. Knit across Needle 1 and Needle 2 in silver (3rd row of stripe). Knit 1 st in silver on Needle 3. Cut off teal from beg of rnd. Beg heel as before with teal on the second st. When the last turn has been made, change to silver, dec with an ssk on the first side, k2tog on the other. Complete 4-row stripe in silver. Cont stripes as established in St st to desired foot length (6 teal-silver stripe repeats), ending with 4 rnds silver.

Toe

Work in teal as for the plain version (page 26), but beg with the instep half of the toe sts, then work the sole half of the toe sts. After the last turn, the RS of the toe bottom will be facing.

Transform Priscilla's Dream Socks into Your Dream Socks

To adapt the pattern for Priscilla's Dream Socks to a different gauge or size, follow the illustration below to figure out your sock circumference measurement, then use that "magic number" to determine all of the other sock measurements and stitch counts, as shown on page 29.

Proportions for an average foot:

Circumference (C) = 100%

Cast-on stitches: 100% of Circumference (adjusted if necessary to be divisible by 4)

Ankle rnds: 20% of Circumference

Heel/toe stitches: 50% of Circumference

Stitches between yarnovers:
20% of Circumference (adjust to closest even number)

Magic length: Circumference minus 1"

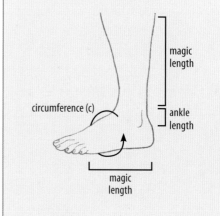

Finishing

With teal threaded on a tapestry needle, use the Kitchener st (see Glossary, page 123) to graft toe to bottom of foot, working the yo tog with the last st. Alternatively, join the sts with the zigzag bind-off used for the plain version.

Gauge (sts per inch)	5	6	7	8	9
C = 5½" (14 cm; child shoe sizes 3–7)					
cast-on sts	28	32	40	44	48
ankle rnds	6	6	8	9	10
heel/toe sts	14	16	20	22	24
sts bet yos	6	6	8	8	10
magic length	4½" (11.5 cm)				
C = 6½" (16.5 cm; child shoe sizes 8–13)					
cast-on sts	32	40	44	52	60
ankle rnds	6	8	9	10	12
heel/toe sts	16	20	22	26	30
sts bet yos	6	8	8	10	12
magic length	5½" (14 cm)				
C = 7½" (19 cm; woman's small)					
cast-on sts	36	44	52	60	68
ankle rnds	7	9	10	12	14
heel/toe sts	18	22	26	30	34
sts bet yos	8	8	10	12	14
magic length	6½" (16.5 cm)				
C = 8" (20.5 cm; woman's medium)					
cast-on sts	40	48	56	64	72
ankle rnds	8	10	11	12	14
heel/toe sts	20	24	28	32	36
sts bet yos	8	10	12	12	14
magic length	7" (18 cm)				

Gauge (sts per inch)	5	6	7	8	9
C = 8½" (21.5 cm; woman's large)					
cast-on sts	44	52	60	68	76
ankle rnds	9	10	12	14	15
heel/toe sts	22	26	30	34	38
sts bet yos	8	10	12	14	16
magic length	7½" (19 cm)				
C = 9" (23 cm; man's small)					
cast-on sts	48	56	64	72	80
ankle rnds	10	11	13	14	16
heel/toe sts	24	28	32	36	40
sts bet yos	10	12	14	14	16
magic length	8" (20.5 cm)				
C = 9½" (24 cm; man's medium)					
cast-on sts	48	56	68	76	84
ankle rnds	10	12	14	15	17
heel/toe sts	24	28	34	38	42
sts bet yos	10	12	14	14	16
magic length	8½" (21.5 cm)				
C = 10" (25.5 cm; man's large)					
cast-on sts	56	60	72	80	88
ankle rnds	12	12	14	16	18
heel/toe sts	28	30	36	40	44
sts bet yos	12	12	14	16	18
magic length	9" (23 cm)				

from the Winter 2005 issue of *Interweave Knits*

Embossed Leaves Socks

Mona Schmidt

Mona Schmidt combined the Embossed Leaves stitch pattern with a smooth two-stranded tubular cast-on, a rib pattern with knit stitches worked through the back loops for crisp definition, to create an elegant sock. The Embossed Leaf pattern is eye-catching, but the subtle details make these socks truly exceptional: The third stitch on each needle grows into a leaf; the unusual garter stitch heel edge extends the purl stitches between the leaves; the star toe completes the leaf motif on its last repeat.

Finished Size
About 7½" (19 cm) foot circumference and 9" (23 cm) foot length. To fit a woman. *Note:* To make the socks larger or smaller, use needles one or two sizes larger or smaller and lengthen or shorten the foot as necessary.

Yarn
Fingering-weight yarn (CYCA #1 Super Fine).
Shown here: Koigu Premium Merino (100% merino wool, 175 yd [160 m]/50 g): #2151 blue-green, 2 skeins.

Needles
Size 2 (2.75 mm): set of 5 double-pointed (dpn). Adjust needle size if necessary to obtain the correct gauge.

Notions
Marker (m); tapestry needle.

Gauge
15 stitches and 22 rounds = 2" (5 cm) in stockinette stitch worked in the round.

Stitch Guide
Twisted Rib: (multiple of 2 sts)
All rnds: *P1, k1 through back loop (tbl); rep from * to end of rnd.

Leaf

Legend:
- ☐ knit
- ⊡ purl
- ╱ k2tog
- ╲ ssk
- ○ yo
- ☐ pattern repeat

Leaf chart (rows 1–15, odd rows numbered on right: 15, 13, 11, 9, 7, 5, 3, 1)

Leg

With 1 dpn and using the 1 × 1 rib method (see Glossary, page 120), CO 64 sts.

Row 1: (WS) K1, *k1 through back loop (k1tbl), sl 1 with yarn in front (wyf); rep from * to last st, k1tbl.

Row 2: *Sl 1 wyf, k1tbl; rep from *.

Arrange sts evenly on 4 dpn (16 sts each needle), place marker (pm), and join for working in the rnd, being careful not to twist sts. Work twisted rib (see Stitch Guide) for 18 rnds—piece should measure about 1¾" (4.5 cm) from CO. Work Rnds 1–16 of Leaf chart across all sts 3 times, then work Rnds 1–8 once more—piece should measure about 6¾" (17 cm) from CO.

Heel

Heel Flap

Work 32 heel sts (all sts on first and second needles) back and forth in rows as foll (rem 32 sts will be worked later for instep):

Row 1: (RS) Knit.

Row 2: (WS) K3, purl to last 3 sts, k3.

Rep these 2 rows 11 more times, ending with a WS row—24 rows total.

Turn Heel

Work short-rows as foll:

Row 1: (RS) K18, k2tog tbl, k1, turn work.

Row 2: (WS) Sl 1 pwise, p5, p2tog, p1, turn.

Row 3: Sl 1 kwise, knit to 1 st before gap formed on previous row, k2tog tbl (1 st each side of gap), k1, turn.

Row 4: Sl 1 pwise, purl to 1 st before gap formed on previous row, p2tog (1 st each side of gap), p1, turn.

Rep Rows 3 and 4 until all heel sts have been worked—18 heel sts rem. Cut yarn.

Shape Gussets

With RS facing, rejoin yarn to beg of right side of heel flap and pick up sts along selvedge edges of heel flap and rejoin for working in the rnd as foll:

Rnd 1: With Needle 1, pick up and knit 15 sts along right edge of heel flap, then k9 heel sts; with Needle 2, k9 rem heel sts, then pick up and knit 15 sts along left edge of flap; with Needle 3, work across first 16 instep sts as established; with Needle 4, work across rem 16 instep sts as established, M1 pwise (see Glossary, page 124)—81 sts total. Rnd begins at center of heel.

Rnd 2: On Needle 1 and Needle 2, knit; on Needle 3 and Needle 4, work sts as established (last st is a purl st).

Rnd 3: On Needle 1, ssk, knit to end; on Needle 2, knit to last 2 sts, k2tog; on Needle 3 and Needle 4, work sts as established—2 sts dec'd.

Rep Rnds 2 and 3 seven more times—65 sts

rem; 16 sts each on Needle 1, Needle 2, and Needle 3; 17 sts on Needle 4.

Foot

Cont in patt as established until Leaf chart has been worked a total of 7 times from CO, then work Rnds 1–8 once more—piece measures about 7½" (19 cm) from back of heel.

Toe

Knit to last 2 sts, k2tog—64 sts rem (16 sts on each needle). Cont as foll:

Rnd 1: *K2, p1, knit to last 2 sts on needle, p2tog; rep from * for rem 3 needles—60 sts rem.

Rnds 2, 4, 6, 8, 10, and 12: Knit.

Rnd 3: *K3, p1, knit to last 2 sts on needle, p2tog; rep from * for rem 3 needles—56 sts rem.

Rnd 5: *K4, p1, knit to last 2 sts on needle, p2tog; rep from * for rem 3 needles—52 sts rem.

Rnd 7: *K5, p1, knit to last 2 sts on needle, p2tog; rep from * for rem 3 needles—48 sts rem.

Rnd 9: *K6, p1, knit to last 2 sts on needle, p2tog; rep from * for rem 3 needles—44 sts rem.

Rnd 11: *K7, p1, knit to last 2 sts on needle, p2tog; rep from * for rem 3 needles—40 sts rem.

Rnd 13: *Knit to last 2 sts on needle, p2tog; rep from * for rem 3 needles—36 sts rem.

Rep Rnd 13 seven more times—8 sts rem.

Finishing

Cut yarn, leaving an 8" (20.5 cm) tail. Thread tail through rem sts, pull snug to tighten, and fasten off. Weave in loose ends. Block lightly.

from the Fall 1999 issue of *Interweave Knits*

JOE COCA

UTE SOCKS

Nancy Bush

These patterned socks were inspired by traditional Ute beadwork. This Native American culture, located west of the Rocky Mountains, is known for highly decorated beaded clothing and accessories. These socks are knitted from cuff to toe, with the two-by-two ribbing at the cuff worked in subtle shades from red to purple. These colors are also used throughout the design, giving a shaded interest to the patterning.

FINISHED SIZE

About 8½ (21.5 cm) foot circumference and 9½" (24 cm) foot length. To fit a woman. *Note:* To make the socks larger or smaller, use needles one or two sizes larger or smaller and lengthen or shorten the foot as necessary.

YARN

Sportweight yarn (CYCA #2 Fine).

Shown here: Brown Sheep NatureSpun Sport (100% wool; 184 yd [168 m]/50 g): #720 ash (tan), #N40 grape harvest (purple), #235 beet red (dark red), #N48 scarlet (bright red), 1 ball each.

NEEDLES

Size 0 (2 mm): set of 5 double-pointed (dpn). Adjust needle size if necessary to obtain the correct gauge.

NOTIONS

Marker (m); tapestry needle.

GAUGE

18 stitches and 22 rounds = 2" (5 cm) in color pattern worked in the round; 16 stitches and 24 rounds = 2" (5 cm) in stockinette stitch worked in the round.

Leg

With scarlet, loosely CO 72 sts. Arrange sts evenly on 4 dpn, place marker (pm), and join for working in the rnd, being careful not to twist sts. Work k2, p2 ribbing for 6 rnds. Join beet red and work 3 rnds as foll: *k2 beet, p2 scarlet; rep from *. With beet only, work 6 rnds in established rib. Join grape harvest and work 3 rnds as foll: *k2 grape, p2 beet; rep from *. With grape only, work 6 rnds in established rib. With ash, knit 3 rnds. Work Rnds 1–56 of Leg chart—piece measures about 7¼" (18.5 cm) from CO.

Heel

Heel Flap

With grape, k18, turn work around. Sl 1 pwise with yarn in front (wyf), p35—36 heel sts centered at back of leg; rem 36 sts will be worked later for instep. Work 36 heel sts back and forth in rows as foll:

Row 1: (RS) *Sl 1 pwise with yarn in back (wyb), k1; rep from *.

Row 2: (WS) Sl 1 pwise wyf, p35.

Rep Rows 1 and 2 until a total of 36 rows have been worked—18 chain sts at each selvedge edge.

Turn Heel

Work short-rows to shape heel as foll:

Row 1: (RS) K20, ssk, k1, turn work.

Row 2: (WS) Sl 1 pwise wyf, p5, p2tog, p1, turn.

Row 3: Sl 1 pwise wyb, knit to 1 st before gap formed on previous row, ssk, k1, turn.

Row 4: Sl 1 pwise wyf, purl to 1 st before gap formed on previous row, p2tog, p1, turn.

Rep Rows 3 and 4 until 20 heel sts rem.

Shape Gussets

Pick up sts along selvedge edges of heel flap and rejoin for working in the rnd as foll: With grape, k10 heel sts; with ash, knit rem 10 heel sts, pick up and knit 18 sts along right side of heel flap, k36 instep sts, pick up and knit 18 sts along left side of heel flap, then knit first 10 heel sts again—92 sts total. Arrange sts so that there are 28 sts on

Foot

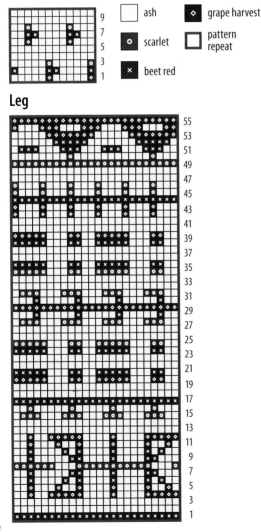

Leg

Needle 1, 18 sts each on Needle 2 and Needle 3, and 28 sts on Needle 4. Rnd begins at center of heel. *Next rnd:* On Needle 1, knit to last 3 sts, k2tog, k1; on Needle 2 and Needle 3, knit; on Needle 4, k1, ssk, knit to end—2 sts dec'd. (*Note:* Always keep the last 3 sts on Needle 1 and the first 3 sts on Needle 4 in ash on all rnds of gusset shaping.) Beg with Rnd 1, work Foot chart as foll:

Rnd 1: On Needle 1, [K1 grape, k5 ash] 4 times, k3 ash; on Needle 2 and Needle 3 (36 sts), [k1 grape, k5 ash] 6 times; on Needle 4, k3 ash, [k1 grape, k5 ash] 4 times.

Rnd 2: On Needle 1, k1 beet, [k4 ash, k2 beet] 3 times, k4 ash, k1 beet, k2tog ash, k1 ash; on Needle 2 and Needle 3, k1 beet, [k4 ash, k2 beet] 5 times, k4 ash, k1 beet; on Needle 4, k1 ash, ssk ash, k1 beet, [k4 ash, k2 beet] 3 times, k4 ash, k1 beet.

Rnd 3: On Needle 1, [k1 scarlet, k5 ash] 4 times, k2 ash; on Needle 2 and Needle 3, [k1 scarlet, k5 ash] 6 times; on Needle 4, k2 ash, [k1 scarlet, k5 ash] 4 times.

Rnd 4: Work with ash as foll: on Needle 1, knit to last 3 sts, k2tog, k1; on Needle 2 and Needle 3, knit; on Needle 4, k1, ssk, knit to end—2 sts dec'd.

Rnds 5 and 9: Knit with ash.

Rnd 6: On Needle 1, k3 ash, [k1 grape, k5 ash] 3 times, k1 grape, k2tog ash, k1 ash; on Needle 2 and Needle 3, k3 ash, [k1 grape, k5 ash] 5 times, k1 grape, k2 ash; on Needle 4, k1 ash, ssk ash, k1 ash, [k1 grape, k5 ash] 3 times, k1 grape, k2 ash—2 sts dec'd.

Rnd 7: On Needle 1, k2 ash, [k2 beet, k4 ash] 3 times, k2 beet, k2 ash; on Needle 2 and Needle 3, k2 ash, [k2 beet, k4 ash] 5 times, k2 beet, k2 ash; on Needle 4, k2 ash, [k2 beet, k4 ash] 3 times, k2 beet, k2 ash.

Rnd 8: On Needle 1, k3 ash, k1 scarlet, [k5 ash, k1 scarlet] 3 times, k2tog ash, k1 ash; on Needle 2 and Needle 3, k3 ash, [k1 scarlet, k5 ash] 5 times, k1 scarlet, k2 ash; on Needle 4, k1 ash, ssk ash, k1 scarlet, [k5 ash, k1 scarlet] 3 times, k2 ash—2 sts dec'd.

Rnd 10: Rep Rnd 4.

Cont in this manner, dec 1 st at end of Needle 1 and beg of Needle 4 every other rnd until 72 sts rem.

Foot

Work even in patt until foot measures about 7½" (19 cm) from back of heel, or about 2" (5 cm) less than desired total foot length.

Toe

With grape, knit 1 rnd. Cont as foll:

Rnd 1: On Needle 1, knit to last 3 sts, k2tog, k1; on Needle 2, k1, ssk, knit to end; on Needle 3, knit to last 3 sts, k2tog, k1; on Needle 4, k1, ssk, knit to end—4 sts dec'd.

Rnd 2: Knit.

Rep Rnds 1 and 2 until 36 sts rem. Rep Rnd 1 *only* until 8 sts rem.

Finishing

Cut yarn, thread tail through rem sts, pull snug to tighten, and fasten off. Weave in loose ends. Block lightly.

from the Summer 2003 issue of *Interweave Knits*

MERINO LACE SOCKS

Anne Woodbury

After reading stitch dictionaries and thinking about Aran sweaters, Anne Woodbury was inspired to combine four complementary eyelet and lace patterns the way that Aran knitting combines cable patterns. Anne worked these socks on two circular needles rather than a set of double-pointed needles, an increasingly popular technique explained below.

FINISHED SIZE

About 8" (20.5 cm) foot circumference and 8¾" (22 cm) foot length. To fit a woman. *Note:* To make the socks larger or smaller, use needles one or two sizes larger or smaller and lengthen or shorten the foot as necessary.

YARN

Fingering-weight yarn (CYCA #1 Super Fine).
Shown here: Koigu Premium Merino (100% Merino; 175 yd [160 m]/50 g): #2501 gray, 3 skeins.

NEEDLES

Size 1 (2.25 mm): two 16" (40 cm) circular (cir). Adjust needle size if necessary to obtain the correct gauge.

NOTIONS

Tapestry needle.

GAUGE

18 stitches and 24 rows = 2" (5 cm) in pattern stitch worked in the round; 14 stitches and 22 rows = 2" (5 cm) in stockinette stitch worked in the round.

NOTE

These socks are worked on two circular needles instead of four or five double-pointed needles, which is more usual.

Working with Two Circular Needles

Cast the required number of sts onto one 16" or 24" (40 or 60 cm) circular (cir) needle. Slide sts to opposite end of needle and slip half of the sts onto another cir needle—Needle 1. Slide sts that rem on Needle 2 to the flexible cable portion of that needle. With sts still on rigid end of Needle 1, hold Needle 1 in front of Needle 2 in preparation for joining into a round. Join the ends, being careful not to twist sts. *Take the opposite tip of Needle 1, bring it around to the right, and knit the sts off the right tip of Needle 1. (Needle 1 will form a circle as sts from the left tip are worked onto the right tip.) When all sts from Needle 1 have been worked, slide them to the flexible cable portion of the needle. Turn the knitting around and pick up Needle 2. Slide the sts from the flexible cable to the right tip of Needle 2. Pick up the left tip of the needle, bring it around and knit the sts on Needle 2. (Needle 2 will form a circle as the sts are worked from one tip to the other.) Slide the sts to the flexible cable portion of Needle 2 and turn the work, returning to Needle 1. Rep from *.

Leg

Using one cir needle, loosely CO 66 sts. Place 33 sts of these sts onto a second cir needle—33 sts each on Needle 1 and Needle 2. Rnd begins at side of leg (bet the two needles). Join for working in the rnd with two cir needles (see box at left), being careful not to twist sts. Work Rnds 1–4 of Rib chart until piece measures 2" (5 cm) from beg. Work Rnds 1–12 of Leg chart 5 times, then work Rnds 1–6 again—piece should measure about 7½" (19 cm) from beg.

Heel

Heel Flap

Slip the first 3 sts from Needle 1 onto Needle 2—30 sts on Needle 1 to be worked for heel; 36 sts on Needle 2 will be worked later for instep. Working 30 heel sts back and forth in rows and slipping the first st of each row pwise with yarn in front (wyf), work Rows 1–12 of Heel chart 2 times, then work Rows 1–6 once more—18 chain sts along each selvedge edge; heel flap measures about 2½" (6.5 cm). Knit 1 (RS) row.

Turn Heel

Work short-rows to shape heel as foll:

Row 1: (WS) P17, p2tog, p1, turn work.

Row 2: (RS) K6, ssk, k1, turn.

Row 3: Purl to 1 st before gap formed on previous row, p2tog (1 st each side of gap), p1, turn.

Row 4: Knit to 1 st before gap formed on previous row, ssk (1 st each side of gap), k1, turn.

Rep Rows 3 and 4 until all sts have been worked, ending with Row 4—18 heel sts rem.

Shape Gussets

Pick up sts along selvedge edges of heel flap and rejoin for working in the rnd as foll:

Rnd 1: With Needle 1, pick up and knit 17 sts along left edge of heel flap; with Needle 2, work 36 instep sts in patt as established (beg with Rnd 1 of Foot chart); with Needle 1, pick up and knit 17 sts along right edge of heel flap, k18 heel sts, cont to end of Needle 1, working left gusset sts again—88 sts total; 52 sts on Needle 1, 36 sts on Needle 2. Work to end of Needle 2. Rnd begins at beg of Needle 1.

Rnd 2: On Needle 1, k1, ssk, knit to last 3 sts, k2tog, k1; on Needle 2, work 36 sts as established—2 sts dec'd.

Rnd 3: Work even in patt.

Rep Rnds 2 and 3 until 30 sts rem on Needle 1—66 sts total.

Foot

Cont as established, working Needle 2 (instep sts) according to Foot chart and Needle 1 (sole sts) in St st until foot measures about 7½" (19 cm) from back of heel, or 2" (5 cm) less than desired total foot length, ending with an even-numbered rnd.

Toe

Change to St st. Knit 1 rnd. Rearrange sts so that there are 33 sts on each needle as foll: Place 2 sts from beg of Needle 2 and 1 st from end of Needle 2 onto Needle 1.

Rnd 1: Knit, dec 1 st at end of each needle as foll: knit to last 3 sts of needle, k2tog, k1; rep from *—32 sts rem each needle.

Rnd 2: On Needle 1, k1, ssk, knit to last 3 sts, k2tog, k1; on Needle 2, k1, ssk, knit to last 3 sts, k2tog, k1—4 sts dec'd.

Rnd 3: Knit.

Rep Rnds 2 and 3 until 36 sts rem (18 sts on each needle). Rep Rnd 2 *every* rnd until 8 sts rem (4 sts on each needle).

Finishing

Cut yarn, leaving a 10" (25.5 cm) tail. Thread tail on tapestry needle and use the Kitchener st (see Glossary, page 123) to graft sts tog. Weave in loose ends. Block lightly.

	knit on RS; purl on WS
•	purl on RS; knit on WS
∕	k2tog
＼	ssk
o	yo
v	sl 1 st pwise with yarn in front
	pattern repeat

Rib

Leg

Heel

Foot

FLAME WAVE SOCKS

Ann Budd

This intriguingly sinuous stitch pattern is paired with a stretchy yarn to create a versatile sock. The resulting socks fit a range of foot sizes and keep their shape. Though the manufacturer of this cotton/elastic blend recommends handwashing and laying the socks flat to dry, we've had success machine-washing ours.

FINISHED SIZE
About 6 (7½)" (15 [18] cm) foot circumference and 7 (8¼)" (18 [21] cm) foot length, unstretched. To fit a child (woman). *Note:* To make the socks larger or smaller, use needles one or two sizes larger or smaller and lengthen or shorten the foot as necessary.

YARN
Sportweight yarn (CYCA #2 Fine).
Shown here: Cascade Fixation (98% cotton, 2% elastic; 186 yd [170 m]/50 g): #5606 olive, 2 balls.

NEEDLES
Upper leg—size 5 (3.75 mm): set of 4 double-pointed (dpn). Lower leg and foot—size 4 (3.5 mm): set of 4 dpn. Adjust needle sizes if necessary to obtain the correct gauge.

NOTIONS
Markers (m); tapestry needle.

GAUGE
12 stitches and 22 rounds = 2" (5 cm) in stockinette stitch worked in the round on size 4 (3.5 mm) needles.

Leg

With size 5 (3.75 mm) needles, loosely CO 42 (56) sts. Arrange sts as evenly as possible on 3 dpn, place marker (pm), and join for working in the rnd, being careful not to twist sts. Rnd begins at back of leg. Knit 1 rnd. Rep Rnds 1–24 of Flame Wave chart until piece measures about 3 (3½)" (7.5 [9] cm) from CO. Change to size 4 (3.5 mm) needles and cont in patt as established until piece measures about 6 (7)" (15 [18] cm) from CO, ending with Rnd 11 or 23 of chart.

Heel

Heel flap

K10 (14), turn work around, sl 1 pwise with yarn in front (wyf), p19 (27)—20 (28) heel sts centered at back of leg; rem 22 (28) sts will be worked later for instep. Work 20 (28) heel sts back and forth in rows as foll:

	knit
╱	k2tog
╲	ssk
M	M1 (see Glossary, page 124)
	pattern repeat

Flame Wave

Row 1: (RS) *Sl 1 kwise with yarn in back (wyb), k1; rep from * to end of row.

Row 2: (WS) Sl 1 pwise with yarn in front (wyf), purl to end.

Rep Rows 1 and 2 until a total of 20 (28) rows have been worked—10 (14) chain sts at each selvedge edge.

Turn Heel

Work short-rows to shape heel as foll:

Row 1: (RS) K12 (16), ssk, k1, turn work.

Row 2: (WS) Sl 1 pwise wyf, p5, p2tog, p1, turn.

Row 3: Sl 1 kwise wyb, knit to 1 st before gap formed on previous row, ssk (1 st from each side of gap), k1, turn.

Row 4: Sl 1 pwise wyf, purl to 1 st before gap formed on previous row, p2tog (1 st from each side of gap), p1, turn.

Rep Rows 3 and 4 until all heel sts have been worked—12 (16) heel sts rem.

Shape Gussets

Pick up sts along sides of heel flap and rejoin for working in the rnd as foll:

Rnd 1: With Needle 1, k12 (16) heel sts, then pick up and knit 11 (15) sts along edge of heel flap; with Needle 2, work across 22 (28) instep sts in patt as established; with Needle 3, pick up and knit 11 (15) sts along other edge of heel flap, then knit the first 6 (8) heel sts from Needle 1 again— 56 (74) sts total; 17 (23) sts each on Needle 1 and Needle 3, 22 (28) instep sts on Needle 2. Rnd begins at center of heel.

Rnd 2: On Needle 1, knit to last 3 sts, k2tog, k1; on Needle 2, work in patt as estab-

lished across center 14 (28) sts, k4 (0); on Needle 3, k1, ssk, knit to end—2 sts dec'd.

Rnd 3: Cont in patt as established (work Needle 2 as charted with 4 (0) sts in St st at each end of needle; work sts on Needle 1 and Needle 3 in St st). Rep Rnds 2 and 3 until 42 (56) sts rem.

Foot

Cont even in patt as established until piece measures about 5¾ (6½)" (14.5 [16.5] cm) from back of heel, or about 1¼ (1¾)" (3.2 [4.5] cm) less than desired total foot length.

Toe

Work in St st as foll:

Rnd 1: On Needle 1, knit to last 2 sts, k2tog; on Needle 2, k1, ssk, knit to last 3 sts, k2tog, k1; on Needle 3, ssk, knit to end—4 sts dec'd.

Rnd 2: Knit.

Rep Rnds 1 and 2 until 22 (28) sts rem. Rep Rnd 1 *every* rnd until 10 (12) sts rem. Knit the sts on Needle 1 onto the end of Needle 3— 5 (6) sts each on 2 needles.

Finishing

Cut yarn, leaving a 12" (30.5 cm) tail. Thread tail on a tapestry needle and use the Kitchener st (see Glossary, page 123) to graft sts tog. Weave in loose ends. Block lightly.

from the Summer 2000 issue of *Spin·Off*

JOE COCA

Two-Yarn Resoleable Socks

Wayne Pfeffer, adapted by Anne Merrow

After knitting many pairs of Elizabeth Zimmermann's Moccasin Socks, Wayne Pfeffer developed this ingenious technique to incorporate a conventional heel flap into a resoleable sock. Placing the heel stitches on a holder, he works the instep for nearly the length of the foot before returning to knit the heel flap, then joins the instep to the sole as it is knitted.

Finished Size

About 9" (23 cm) foot circumference and 11" (28 cm) foot length. To fit a man.

Yarn

Worsted-weight yarn (CYCA #4 Medium).
Shown here: Brown Sheep Lamb's Pride Superwash (100% wool; 200 yd [183 m]/100 g): #SW150 stonewashed denim (light blue; MC) and #SW175 blue diamond (medium blue; CC), 1 ball each.

Needles

Size 4 (3.5 mm)—two sets of 5 double-pointed (dpn). *Note:* Two circular needles (cir) are optional, but may be helpful.

Notions

Tapestry needle; stitch holders; point protectors (optional) to prevent sts from falling off dpn.

Gauge

12 stitches and 15½ rounds = 2" (5 cm) in stockinette stitch worked in the round.

Notes

- If you use a sportweight yarn (CYCA #2 Fine) and smaller needles to get a gauge of 7 stitches per inch (2.5 cm), these instructions will produce socks with about an 8" (20.5 cm) foot circumference. Work as many rows/rounds as needed using your substitute yarn and needles to match the length measurements given.

- Although the pair shown here uses the same yarn for the sole and instep, Wayne's original pattern used a sturdy yarn for the heel and sole and a soft yarn for the cuff and instep. The heel and sole can be replaced if they wear out, but using durable yarn may keep these socks in use for a long time. Wayne suggests "Tuffy" by Briggs & Little.

Leg

With MC, loosely CO 60 sts. Arrange sts evenly on 4 dpn so that there are 15 sts each needle. Place marker (pm) and join for working in the rnd, being careful not to twist sts. Work k2, p2 rib for 9 rnds—piece measures about 1" (2.5 cm) from CO. Change to CC and work 4 rnds in established rib. Change to MC and work 2 more rnds—15 rnds rib completed; piece measures about 1¾" (4.5 cm) from CO. Change to St st and work even until piece measures 8" (20.5 cm) from CO, or desired length to top of heel.

Instep

Place next 29 sts on a holder for the heel. Turn work so WS is facing and p31—31 sts for instep. Work back and forth in rows in St st as foll, beg with a RS row:

Rows 1 and 2: Work even in patt. *Note:* Work the edge sts on every row; do not slip the selvedge sts.

Row 3: (RS) K1, ssk, work in patt to last 3 sts, k2tog, k1—29 sts rem.

Rows 4–6: Work even in patt.

Row 7: Repeat Row 3—27 sts rem.

Row 8: Work even in patt.

Rows 9–54: Work 46 rows even in patt, and *at the same time* sl the first st of every RS row as if to knit with yarn in back (kwise wyb), and sl the first st of every WS row as if to purl with yarn in front (pwise wyf)—piece measures about 7" (18 cm) from beg of instep, or about 4" (10 cm) less than desired total foot length. Place

sts on holder. Cut yarn, leaving a 12"
(30.5 cm) tail.

Sole Preparation

Note: In preparation for joining the instep
and sole, you will establish live sts around
all three sides of the instep rectangle using
3 dpn, picking up sts along one selvedge of
the instep, working across the live sts at the
end of the instep, then picking up sts along
the other instep selvedge. The heel sts are
worked using a fourth dpn. You may find
it helpful to use 6 dpn instead of 4, using 2
separate needles to hold the sts along each
selvedge of the instep. (The pair shown here
was made using 2 cir needles, using 1 to hold
sts from around the three sides of the instep,
and the other to work the heel and sole,
joining the sides of the sole to the instep by
working sts tog at each end of every row.)

JOE COCA

With RS of instep facing you, join CC to beg of RS of instep Row 1, in the corner where the instep meets the held heel sts.

Rnd 1: With Needle 1, M1 (see Glossary, page 124) in corner between heel and instep sts, pick up and knit 5 sts from the first 8 instep rows, then pick up and knit 23 sts from the next 46 instep rows, picking up the outside loop of each slipped selvedge st—29 sts on Needle 1. Return 27 held instep sts to dpn, and with Needle 2, knit across 27 instep sts— 27 sts on Needle 2. With Needle 3, pick up and knit 23 sts from next 46 instep rows as foll: pick up the outside loop of each slipped selvedge st, pick up and knit 5 sts from the first 8 instep rows, M1 in corner between instep and heel sts—

Resoling this Sock

If the bottom of the foot ever wears out, snip the grafting at the end of the toe, and unravel the toe, sole, and heel. If the foot has holes and cannot be unraveled in one piece, carefully snip the CC from the first sole preparation rnd in several places, pick out the yarn from that rnd all the way around between the snips, and the bottom of the foot will fall off. Carefully unravel the rest of the sole to expose the live sts for the end of the instep and beg of the heel, and place these live sts on needles or stitch holders, then knit an entirely new heel, sole, and toe.

29 sts on Needle 3. Return 29 held heel sts to dpn, and with Needle 4, k15 heel sts, M1, k14 heel sts—30 sts on Needle 4; 115 sts total.

Rnd 2: Knit, working any loose sts from the last rnd through their back loops (tbl) if necessary to tighten them.

You may wish to put point protectors on Needles 1, 2, and 3, or place the 85 sts from these needles on stitch holders as you work the heel.

Heel

Heel Flap

Turn work so WS is facing. With CC, sl 1 pwise wyf, p29.

Work 30 heel sts on Needle 4 back and forth in rows as foll:

Row 1: (RS) *Sl 1 kwise wyb, k1; rep from *.

Row 2: (WS) Sl 1 pwise wyf, purl to end.

Rep Rows 1 and 2 until a total of 24 rows have been worked—12 chain sts along each selvedge; heel flap measures about 2½" (6.5 cm).

Turn Heel

Work short-rows to shape heel as foll:

Row 1: (RS) Sl 1 pwise wyb, k15, ssk, k1, turn work.

Row 2: (WS) Sl 1 pwise wyf, p3, p2tog, p1, turn.

Row 3: Sl 1 kwise wyb, knit to 1 st before gap formed on previous row, ssk (1 st from each side of gap), k1, turn.

Row 4: Sl 1 pwise wyf, purl to 1 st before gap formed on previous row, p2tog (1 st from each side of gap), p1, turn.

Rep Rows 3 and 4 until all heel sts have been worked—16 heel sts rem. Cont in this manner, working 1 more st before dec every row, until 14 sts rem. *Next row:* (RS) Ssk, knit to last 2 sts, k2tog—14 sts. Do not cut yarn.

Shape Gussets and Begin Sole

If necessary, return 85 held sts of sole preparation to dpns or single cir needle. With RS still facing, cont as foll with CC, picking up sts from slipped heel flap selvedges through their outside loops:

Row 1: (RS) Pick up and knit 12 sts along edge of heel flap, sl last picked-up st to needle holding instep sts, ssk last heel st tog with first instep st, turn.

Row 2: (WS) Sl 1 pwise wyf, p25 to end of heel sts, pick up and purl (see Glossary, page 125) 12 sts along other edge of heel flap, sl last picked-up st to needle holding instep sts, p2tog (last heel st and first instep st), turn—38 sts total for heel and gussets; 1 st joined from each end of instep sts. Sole is now worked back and forth on sts of heel and gussets.

Row 3: Sl 1 pwise wyb, ssk, knit to last 3 sole sts, k2tog, ssk last sole st with next instep st, turn—36 sole sts rem.

Row 4: Sl 1 pwise wyf, purl to last sole st, p2tog last st with next instep st, turn.

Repeat Rows 3 and 4 four more times—28 sole sts rem.

Continue Sole

Cont with CC as foll:

Row 1: Sl 1 pwise wyb, knit to last sole st, ssk last sole st with next instep st, turn.

Row 2: Sl 1 pwise wyf, purl to last sole st, p2tog last sole st with next instep st, turn.

Rep the last 2 rows until all sts from selvedges of instep have been joined; *do not* join any sole sts to 27 sts on needle at end of instep—55 sts rem; 28 sts for sole, 27 sts for end of instep.

Toe

With CC, k28 sole sts, k14 instep sts, M1, k13 instep sts—56 sts. Arrange sts evenly on 4 dpn so that there are 14 sts on each needle. Pm to indicate beg of rnd at start of sole sts. If necessary, work even in St st in the rnd until piece measures about 9" (23 cm) from back of heel, or 2" (5 cm) less than desired total foot length. Shape toe as foll:

Rnd 1: On Needle 1, knit to last 3 sts, k2tog, k1; on Needle 2, k1, ssk, knit to last 3 sts, k2tog, k1; on Needle 3, k1, ssk, knit to end—4 sts dec'd.

Rnd 2: Knit.

Repeat Rnds 1 and 2 until 16 sts rem. Arrange sts on 2 needles with 8 sts each for top and bottom of toe.

Finishing

Cut yarn, leaving a 12" (30.5 cm) tail. Thread tail on a tapestry needle and use the Kitchener st (see Glossary, page 123) to graft sts tog. Weave in loose ends. Block lightly.

from the Winter 2000 issue of *Interweave Knits*

AUSTRIAN SOCKS

Candace Eisner Strick

Candace Eisner Strick drew on her love of traditional Austrian textural patterns to create these bold socks. She combined the stitch motifs *Doppelviereck mit Drahdi* ("double squares with cables") and *Ketterl* ("little chains") to form the seemingly complex sculptural work on the legs. The pattern is easier to master than it appears, as it uses a simple twisted-stitch technique rather than the cable needle knitters might expect. The cuffs are begun by knitting I-cord to encircle the calf, from which stitches are picked up to knit the leg.

FINISHED SIZE

About 8½" (21.5 cm) foot circumference and 9" (23 cm) foot length. To fit a woman. *Note:* To make the socks larger or smaller, use needles one or two sizes larger or smaller and lengthen or shorten the foot as necessary.

YARN

Sportweight yarn (CYCA #2 Fine).
Shown here: Gems Opal (100% merino; 225 yd [205 m]/100 g): #30 off-white, 2 skeins.

NEEDLES

Size 2 (2.75 mm): set of 4 double-pointed (dpn). Adjust needle size if necessary to obtain the correct gauge.

NOTIONS

Small amount of waste yarn; markers (m); tapestry needle.

GAUGE

12 stitches and 19 rounds = 2" (5 cm) in stockinette stitch worked in the round.

Stitch Guide

K1tbl
Knit 1 through back loop.

P1tbl
Purl 1 through back loop.

Right Traveler (worked over 2 sts)
Work to the purl st before the k1tbl symbol and sl the next 2 sts kwise (a purl st and a knit st). Insert the tip of the left needle into the back of the second st on right needle, pull the right needle out of these 2 sts, letting the first st fall free in front of work. Immediately pick up the free st with the right needle and place it back on the left needle—the 2 sts have exchanged places—work them as k1, p1.

Left Traveler (worked over 2 sts)
Work to the k1tbl symbol and sl the next 2 sts pwise (a knit st and a purl st). Insert the tip of the left needle into the front of the second st on right needle, pull the right needle out of these 2 sts, letting the first st fall free in back of work. Immediately pick up the free st with the right needle and place it on the left needle—the 2 sts have exchanged places—work them as p1, k1tbl.

Right Cross (worked over 2 sts)
Sl 2 kwise, complete as for right traveler, working the 2 exchanged sts as k2.

Left Cross (worked over 2 sts)
Sl 2 pwise, complete as for left traveler, working the 2 exchanged sts as [k1tbl] 2 times.

Band Pattern (worked over 9 sts)
Set-up row: K1tbl, [k1tbl, p1] 3 times, [k1tbl] 2 times.

Row 1: [K1tbl] 2 times, p1, k1tbl, work next 2 sts as foll: sl 2 kwise, insert tip of left needle into back of second st on right needle, pull right needle out of these 2 sts so that the first st falls free in front of work, pick up free st with right needle and place on left needle (the 2 sts have exchanged places), k2, p1, [k1tbl] 2 times.

Row 2: [K1tbl] 2 times, p1, work next 2 sts as foll: sl 2 kwise, insert tip of left needle into the back of second st on right needle, pull right needle out of these 2 sts so that first st falls free in front of work, pick up free st with right needle and place on left needle (the 2 sts have exchanged places), k1, p1, k1tbl, p1, [k1tbl] 2 times.

Repeat Rows 1 and 2 for pattern.

Notes

- *Überlieferte Strickmuster aus dem Steirischen Ennstal* (Traditional Knitting Patterns from the Enns Valley of Styria) by Maria Erlbacher is available from Schoolhouse Press.

- The twisted knit stitches travel over the purl stitches on every round. This is accomplished by slipping 2 stitches and having them exchange places.

- In this pattern, right travelers are slipped as if to knit, which puts a twist into the stitch; they are then knitted through the fronts to keep this twist, making right-slanting stitches. The left travelers are slipped as if to purl; they are then knitted through the backs, making them left-slanting stitches. The resulting stitches are mirror images of each other and perfectly balanced.

Leg

Band

With waste yarn and using a provisional method (see Glossary, page 121), CO 9 sts. Purl 1 row. Work these 9 sts as I-cord (see Glossary, page 124) for 72 rows. The loops of yarn across the back of work will be noticeable, but they are useful for keeping track of the number of rows worked. (*Note:* The first and last sts will roll under to form rounded edges. The band will twist as you go but will straighten out when sts are picked up later for the leg.) Carefully remove waste yarn from provisional CO and place 9 live sts onto a separate dpn. With yarn threaded on a tapestry needle, use the Kitchener st (see Glossary, page 123) to graft live sts tog, forming a ring.

Leg

With RS facing and beg 18 sts to right of graft, pick up and knit 72 sts around band, working into the back loop of each st on the band edge. Arrange sts evenly on 3 dpn, place marker (pm), and join for working in the rnd. Rnd begs at outside of leg. Beg with set-up rnd, work 36 sts of Leg chart 2 times. Work Rnds 1–14 three times, then work Rnds 1–7 once more.

Heel

Heel Flap

The heel is worked back and forth on the first 36 sts of rnd; rem 36 sts will be worked later for instep.

Row 1: (RS) *Sl 1 pwise with yarn in back (wyb), k1; rep from * and *at the same time* dec 4 sts evenly spaced—32 sts rem.

Row 2: (WS) Sl 1 pwise with yarn in front (wyf), purl to end.

Row 3: *Sl 1 pwise wyb, k1; rep from *. Rep Rows 2 and 3 until a total of 24 rows have been worked, ending with Row 2— 12 chain sts along each selvedge edge.

Turn Heel

Work short-rows to shape heel as foll:

Row 1: (RS) K18, sl 1, k1, psso, k1, turn work.

Row 2: (WS) Sl 1 pwise wyf, p5, p2tog, p1, turn.

Row 3: Knit to 1 st before gap formed on previous row, sl 1, k1, psso, k1, turn.

Row 4: Sl 1, purl to 1 st before gap formed on previous row, p2tog (1 st each side of gap), p1, turn.

Rep Rows 3 and 4 until all sts have been worked, ending with a WS row.

Shape Gussets

Pick up sts along selvedge edges of heel flap and rejoin for working in the rnd as foll:

Rnd 1: With Needle 1, knit heel sts then pick up and knit 12 sts along side of heel flap; with Needle 2, work Rnd 8 of chart across 36 instep sts; with Needle 3, pick up and knit 12 sts along other side of heel flap then knit first 9 heel sts from Needle 1 again—78 sts total. Rnd begins at center of heel.

Rnd 2: On Needle 1, knit to last 3 sts, k2tog, p1; on Needle 2, work Rnd 9 of Leg chart across 36 sts; on Needle 3, p1, ssk, knit to end—2 sts dec'd.

Rnd 3: On Needle 1, knit to last st, p1; on Needle 2, work in patt as established; on

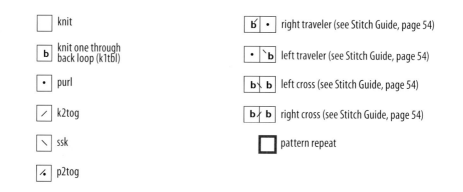

	knit
b	knit one through back loop (k1tbl)
•	purl
╱	k2tog
╲	ssk
⟋	p2tog

b́ •	right traveler (see Stitch Guide, page 54)
• **b**	left traveler (see Stitch Guide, page 54)
b **b**	left cross (see Stitch Guide, page 54)
b **b**	right cross (see Stitch Guide, page 54)
	pattern repeat

Leg

13
11
9
7
5
3
1 set-up round

Toe

21
19
17
15
13
11

Needle 3, p1, knit to end.
Rep Rnds 2 and 3 until 68 sts rem—16 sts each on Needle 1 and Needle 3; 36 instep sts on Needle 2.

Foot

Work even as established through Rnd 14 of chart, then work Rnds 1–14 two more times, then work Rnds 1–10 once more—piece measures about 7¼" (18.5 cm) from back of heel.

Toe

Work sts on Needle 1 and Needle 3 in St st and work sts on Needle 2 as foll:

Rnd 1: On Needle 1, knit to last 3 sts, k2tog, k1; on Needle 2, work Rnd 11 of Toe chart; on Needle 3, k1, ssk, knit to end—60 sts rem.

Rnd 2: On Needle 1, knit; on Needle 2, work Rnd 12 of chart; on Needle 3, knit.

Rnd 3: On Needle 1, knit to last 3 sts, k2tog, k1; on Needle 2, work Rnd 13 of chart; on Needle 3, k1, ssk, knit to end—56 sts rem.

Rnd 4: Rep Rnd 2 on Needle 1 and Needle 3; work Rnd 14 of chart on Needle 2.

Rep Rnds 3 and 4 until Rnd 18 of chart has been completed—24 sts rem on Needle 2. On Needles 1 and 3 work Rnd 3 *only* (dec every rnd) until Toe chart has been completed. Cont working all sts in St st and dec every rnd as established until 8 sts rem—2 sts each on Needle 1 and Needle 3; 4 sts on Needle 2. Knit sts on Needle 1 onto Needle 3—4 sts each on 2 needles.

Finishing

Cut yarn, leaving 12" (30.5 cm) tail. Thread tail on tapestry needle and use the Kitchener st (see Glossary, page 123) to graft sts tog. Weave in loose ends. Block lightly.

from the Summer 2005 issue of *Interweave Knits*

PADDED FOOTLETS

Mary Snyder

Indulge your feet with Mary Snyder's short socks knitted with a double thickness of yarn to cushion the soles. The padding is worked in a sequence of two rounds that uses two strands of yarn for the sole stitches and a single strand for the instep stitches. The transition between the padded sole and single-thickness instep is cleverly concealed along a column of purl stitches. Little touches—a lace panel on the instep that's repeated on the heel flap, ankle-hugging ribbing, and a trim accent stripe on the cuff and toe—give the footlets a polished look.

FINISHED SIZE
About 7" (18 cm) foot circumference, unstretched, 8" (20.5 cm) circumference comfortably stretched, and about 10" (25.5 cm) foot length. To fit a woman.

YARN
Fingering-weight yarn (CYCA #1 Super Fine).
Shown here: Gems Pearl (100% superwash merino; 185 [169 m]/50 g): #50 sage (MC), 2 skeins, and #02 tobacco (CC), 1 skein.

NEEDLES
Size 0 (2 mm): set of 5 double-pointed (dpn). Adjust needle size if necessary to obtain the correct gauge.

NOTIONS
Marker (m); tapestry needle.

GAUGE
14 stitches and 22 rows = 2" (5 cm) in stockinette stitch worked in the round.

STITCH GUIDE
Wrap next stitch, turn
With yarn in front, slip the next stitch as if to purl, bring yarn to back, and turn work. On the following row, slip the wrapped stitch as if to purl with yarn in front.

NOTE
When working the heel flap and turning the heel, slip the first st as if to knit with yarn in back on both right-side and wrong-side rows.

Leg
Cuff
With MC and using the long-tail method (see Glossary, page 120), CO 58 sts. Arrange sts on 4 dpn, place marker (pm), and join for working in the rnd, being careful not to twist sts. With MC and beg with p1, work p1, k1 rib for 2 rnds. With CC, knit 1 rnd, then work 1 rnd in p1, k1 rib as before. Cut off CC. Cont with MC only, knit 1 rnd, then work p1, k1 rib for 6 rnds.

Shape back of ankle
Work back and forth in short-rows (see Glossary, page 125) as foll:

Row 1: (RS) [P1, k1] 14 times, wrap next st, turn (see Stitch Guide).

Row 2: (WS) Sl 1 (wrapped st) pwise, [p1, k1] 13 times, p1, wrap next st (first st of original rnds), turn.

Row 3: Sl 1 pwise, [k1, p1] 13 times, wrap next st, turn.

Row 4: Sl 1 pwise, [k1, p1] 12 times, k1, wrap next st (second st of original rnds), turn.

Row 5: Sl 1 pwise, [p1, k1] 12 times, p1, pick up and knit the next wrap tog with the previously slipped knit st, pick up and purl the foll wrap tog with the previously slipped purl st, then work established rib to end-of-rnd marker (m)—2 wrapped sts rem at beg of next rnd, after marker.

Heel
Heel Flap
Work heel flap back and forth in rows on the first 29 sts as foll: *Set-up row:* Pick up and knit the next wrap tog with the previously slipped purl st, pick up and knit the foll wrap tog with the previously slipped knit st, k3, k2tog, k1, yo, p1, k11, p1, yo, k1, ssk, k4, p1— 29 sts. Turn. Change to Heel Flap chart and work Rows 2–10 once (set-up rnd counts as Row 1 of first patt rep), then work Rows 1–10 once, then work Rows 1–9 once more. Join a second strand of MC. *Next row:* (WS) With 2 strands held tog, sl 1 kwise, p28. *Next row:* Sl 1 kwise, k27, p1. Rep the last 2 rows 2 more times then work WS row once more.

Turn Heel
Cont with yarn doubled, work short-rows as foll:

Row 1: (RS) Sl 1 kwise, k16, ssk, p1, turn work.

Row 2: Sl 1 kwise, p6, p2tog, p1, turn.

Row 3: Sl 1 kwise, k7, ssk, p1, turn.

Row 4: Sl 1 kwise, p8, p2tog, p1, turn.

Cont in this manner, working 1 more st before dec until every st has been worked, ending with a WS row—17 sts rem.

Shape Gussets
Establish instep gussets, lace instep panel, and padded sole as foll:

Rnd 1: Cont with yarn doubled, sl 1 kwise, k16, pick up and knit 1 st in each of the next 5 selvedge sts of heel flap, drop 1 strand to the inside of the sock, cont with a single strand of yarn and pick up and knit 14 more sts along side heel flap to beg of instep sts, pm, work 29 instep sts according to Rnd 1 of Instep chart, pm, pick up and knit 14 sts along side of heel flap, pm, pick up and knit 5 more sts along heel flap, ending at beg of heel sts—84 sts total. Rearrange sts so first

- knit on RS; purl on WS
- purl on RS; knit on WS
- k2tog
- ssk
- yo
- sl 1 (see Note)

Heel Flap

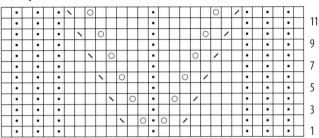

Instep

22 and last 5 sts of rnd are on the first needle for sole (27 sole sts total), 14 sts each on 2 needles for gussets, and 29 sts on single needle for instep. Working yarn is between the 5th and 6th sts on the sole needle.

Rnd 2: With single strand of working yarn, *sl 1 pwise with yarn in back (wyb), k1; rep from * to last 2 sts of sole needle, sl 1 pwise wyb, p1, drop current working yarn, turn work. With WS facing, pick up yarn dropped on previous rnd and cont as foll: *Sl 1 pwise with yarn in front (wyf), p1; rep from * to last st of sole needle, drop working strand to outside of work (this strand will be 1 of 2 strands used for the sole in the next row), sl 1 pwise, turn. With RS facing, skip to the end of the sole needle without working the sole sts again, pick up the single strand of yarn dropped there, and cont across the gusset and instep sts as foll: Knit to 3 sts before beg of instep, k2tog, k1; on instep needle work 29 instep sts according to next row of Instep chart; k1, ssk, knit to end—2 sts dec'd; both strands of yarn are at beg of sole needle.

Rnd 3: There will be 1 strand coming from in front of the first sole needle, and 1 strand coming from between the first and second sts on the sole needle. Holding both strands together, p1 tightly, cont with double strand, knit to last st of sole needle, p1, drop 1 strand to inside of work, cont with single strand, knit sts of first gusset, work 29 instep sts according to next row of Instep chart, knit sts of second gusset.

Rnd 4: With single strand, p1, *sl 1 pwise wyb, k1; rep from * to last 2 sts of sole needle, sl 1 pwise wyb, p1, drop current working yarn, turn. With WS facing, pick up strand dropped on previous rnd and cont as foll: *Sl 1 pwise wyf, p1; rep from * to last st of sole needle, drop working strand to outside of work, sl 1 pwise, turn. With RS facing, skip to the end of the sole needle without working the sole sts again, pick up the single strand of yarn dropped there and knit sts of first gusset, work 29 instep sts according to next row of Instep chart, knit sts of second gusset; both strands of yarn are at beg of sole needle.

Rnd 5: Rep Rnd 3.

Cont instep sts in patt from chart, rep the shaping of Rnds 2–5 eleven more times, redistributing sts as necessary when number of sts becomes too few to grip needles securely, and ending with Rnd 1 of chart—60 sts rem; 27 sole sts, 29 instep sts, 2 knit sts for each gusset; 49 chart rnds completed to end with Rnd 1 of Instep chart. Cont instep sts in patt from chart, work Rnd 2 once more, working gusset decs as k2tog over 2 sts of first gusset, and ssk over 2 sts of second gusset—58 sts rem; 27 sole sts, 29 instep sts, 1 knit st for each gusset.

Foot

Redistribute sts again, if desired, and rep Rnds 3 and 4 until Instep chart has been worked 5 times total, ending with Rnd 12 of chart and Rnd 4 of padded sole patt—foot measures about 8" (20.5 cm) from back of heel. For a longer foot, rep Rnds 3 and 4 of padded sole, working instep sts in St st, until foot measures 2" (5 cm) shorter than desired total length, ending with Rnd 4.

Toe

Cont working padding on sole sts only, work the first and last sole sts and sts for the top of toe with a single strand of yarn as foll:

Rnd 1: With MC, k1 with single strand, cont with double strand, knit to last sole st, drop 1 strand to inside of work, cont with single strand, knit last sole st, knit to end.

Rnd 2: With single strand of CC, k1, *sl 1 pwise wyb, k1; rep from * to last 2 sole sts, sl 1 pwise wyb, k1, drop CC working yarn, turn. With WS facing, join a new strand of CC and cont as foll: *Sl 1 pwise wyf, p1; rep from * to last st of sole needle, drop working strand to outside of work, sl 1 pwise, turn. With RS facing, skip to the end of the sole needle without working the sole sts again, pick up the single strand of CC dropped there, and knit to end; both strands of yarn are at end of rnd.

Rnd 3: With CC, rep Rnd 1.

Rnd 4: With single strand of CC, k1, *sl 1 pwise wyb, k1; rep from * to last 2 sole sts, sl 1 pwise wyb, k1, drop CC working yarn, turn. With WS facing, pick up strand

of CC dropped on previous row and cont as foll: *Sl 1 pwise wyf, p1; rep from * to last sole st, drop working strand to outside of work, sl 1 pwise, turn. With RS facing, skip to the end of the sole needle without working the sole sts again, pick up the single strand of CC dropped there, and knit to end; both strands of yarn are at end of rnd. Cut CC and cont with MC to end.

Rnd 5: Rep Rnd 1.

Rnd 6: With MC, rep Rnd 2, dec 4 sts as foll: On sole sts work k1, ssk, work in patt to last 3 sole sts, k2tog, k1; on top of toe sts work k1, ssk, knit to last 3 top of toe sts, k2tog, k1—4 sts dec'd.

Rnds 7–22: Rep Rnds 3 and 4 with MC, dec 4 sts as in Rnd 6 on Rnds 10, 13, 16, 18, 20, 21, and 22—26 sts rem.

Finishing

Cut yarn, leaving a 20" (51 cm) tail. Divide sts evenly on two needles. With yarn threaded on a tapestry needle, use the Kitchener st (see Glossary, page 123) to graft sts tog. Weave in loose ends. Block lightly.

Mock Wave Cable Socks

Ann Budd

Ann Budd designed these classic socks to have the look of cables without the bulk. The cable-like waves are created with an easy-to-memorize pattern of knit and purl stitches that "travel" with increases and decreases paired on the same row. The slightly rugged look is appropriate for a man or woman.

FINISHED SIZE
About 6 (8)" (15 [20.5] cm) foot circumference and 7½ (9½)" (19 [24] cm) foot length. To fit a child (adult). *Note:* To make the socks larger or smaller, use needles one or two sizes larger or smaller and lengthen or shorten the foot as necessary.

YARN
Fingering-weight yarn (CYCA #1 Super Fine).
Shown here: Zitron Trekking Tweed XXL (75% wool, 25% nylon; 462 yd [422 m]/100 g): #250 Blue tweed, 1 ball.

NEEDLES
Upper leg—size 3 (3.25 mm): set of 4 double-pointed (dpn). Lower leg and foot—size 2 (2.75 mm): set of 4 dpn. Adjust needle sizes if necessary to obtain the correct gauge.

NOTIONS
Marker (m); tapestry needle.

GAUGE
18 stitches and 24 rounds = 2" (5 cm) in stockinette stitch worked in the round on smaller needles for lower leg and foot.

Leg

With size 3 (3.25 mm) needles and using the old Norwegian method (see Glossary, page 121), CO 60 (80) sts. Arrange sts as evenly as possible on 3 dpn, place marker (pm), and join for working in the rnd, being careful not to twist sts. Knit 1 rnd. Rep Rnds 1–16 of Mock Wave Cable chart until piece measures 2¾ (4)" (7 [10] cm) from CO. Change to size 2 (2.75 mm) needles and cont in patt from chart until piece measures about 5½ (7½)" (14 [19] cm) from CO, ending with Rnd 8 or 16 of chart.

Heel
Heel Flap

K10 (20), turn work so WS is facing, sl 1 pwise with yarn in front (wyf), p29 (39)— 30 (40) heel sts approximately centered over patt on back of leg; rem 30 (40) sts will be worked later for instep. Work 30 (40) heel sts back and forth in rows as foll:

Row 1: (RS) *Sl 1 kwise with yarn in back (wyb), k1; rep from * to end of row.

Row 2: (WS) Sl 1 pwise with wyf, purl to end.

Rep Rows 1 and 2 until a total of 30 (40) rows have been worked—15 (20) chain sts along each selvedge edge.

Turn Heel

Work short-rows to shape heel as foll:

Row 1: (RS) K17 (22), ssk, k1, turn work.

Row 2: (WS) Sl 1, p5, p2tog, p1, turn.

Row 3: Sl 1, knit to 1 st before gap formed on previous row, ssk (1 st from each side of gap), k1, turn.

Row 4: Sl 1, purl to 1 st before gap formed on previous row, p2tog (1 st from each side of gap), p1, turn.

Rep Rows 3 and 4 until all heel sts have been worked—18 (22) heel sts rem.

knit

• purl

⁄ k2tog

＼ ssk

M M1 (see Glossary, page 124)

pattern repeat

Mock Wave Cable

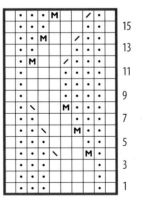

Shape Gussets

Pick up sts along selvedge edges of heel flap and rejoin for working in the rnd as foll:

Rnd 1: With Needle 1, k18 (22) heel sts then pick up and knit 16 (21) sts along edge of heel flap; with Needle 2, work across 30 (40) instep sts in patt as established; with Needle 3, pick up and knit 16 (21) sts along other edge of heel flap then knit the first 9 (11) heel sts from Needle 1 again—80 (104) sts total; 25 (32) sts each on Needle 1 and Needle 3; 30 (40) instep sts on Needle 2. Rnd begins at center of heel.

Rnd 2: On Needle 1, knit to last 3 sts, k2tog, k1; on Needle 2, work in patt as established; on Needle 3, k1, ssk, knit to end—2 sts dec'd.

Rnd 3: Cont in patt as established (work sts on Needle 2 in patt from chart; work sts on Needle 1 and Needle 3 in St st).

Rep Rnds 2 and 3 until 60 (80) sts rem.

Foot

Cont even in patt as established until piece measures about 6 (7½)" (15 [19] cm) from back of heel, or about 1½ (2)" (3.8 [5] cm) less than desired total foot length.

Toe

Work in St st as foll:

Rnd 1: On Needle 1, knit to last 2 sts, k2tog, k1; on Needle 2, k1, ssk, knit to last 3 sts, k2tog, k1; on Needle 3, k1, ssk, knit to end—4 sts dec'd.

Rnd 2: Knit.

Rep Rnds 1 and 2 until 32 (40) sts rem. Rep Rnd 1 *every* rnd until 12 (16) sts rem. Knit the sts on Needle 1 onto the end of Needle 3—6 (8) sts each on 2 needles.

Finishing

Cut yarn, leaving a 12" (30.5 cm) tail. Thread tail on a tapestry needle and use the Kitchener st (see Glossary, page 123) to graft sts tog. Weave in loose ends. Block lightly.

JOE COCA

from the Spring 1997 issue of *Interweave Knits*

Meida's Socks

Nancy Bush

On her first visit to Estonia, Nancy Bush received a pair of lacy socks from her friend Meida Joeveer, who explained how she had made them. Nancy studied the socks and has reproduced them here. Alternating slipped stitches on every right-side row produces a reinforced heel flap with a honeycomb rather than the usual rib, which continues into the turning of the heel. The only change from the original pattern is a wedge toe, with decreases worked every other round to add length to the foot. The remaining eight toe stitches are drawn up into a "rosebud."

FINISHED SIZE
About 7½" (19 cm) foot circumference and 9½" (24 cm) foot length. To fit a woman. *Note:* To make the socks larger or smaller, use needles one or two sizes larger or smaller and lengthen or shorten the foot as necessary.

YARN
Sportweight yarn (CYCA #2 Fine).
Shown here: Stahl Wolle Olé (51% cotton, 49% wool; 125 yd (115m)/50 g): #1604 cream, 2 balls (3 balls if you lengthen the socks). *Note:* This yarn has been discontinued; substitute the sportweight yarn of your choice.

NEEDLES
Size 1 (2.25 mm): set of 5 double-pointed (dpn). Adjust needle size if necessary to obtain the correct gauge.

NOTIONS
Marker (m); cable needle (cn); tapestry needle.

GAUGE
11 stitches and 16 rows = 2" (5 cm) in stockinette stitch worked in the round.

Estonian Cables

In Estonia, where cable needles are not common, the cable action is performed on the four stitches (numbered 1, 2, 3 and 4, with stitch #1 closest to the left needle point and stitch #4 the farthest away) as follows: Put the right needle into the back of #3 and #4. Pull the left needle out of all 4 sts, leaving #1 and #2 in mid air for a moment. Place #2, then #1 on the left needle, then place #4, then #3 onto the left needle. Knit #3 and #4, then put the right needle into the back of #2 (now in #4's original position) and slip the left needle out of #2 and #1, just as you did with #3 and #4 before. Stitch #1 will be in mid air for a moment. Place #1 then #2 on the left needle and knit each of them.

Lace

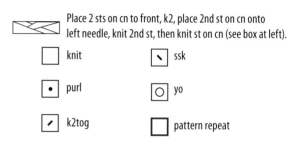

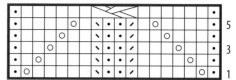 Place 2 sts on cn to front, k2, place 2nd st on cn onto left needle, knit 2nd st, then knit st on cn (see box at left).

☐ knit   ◥ ssk

• purl   Ⓞ yo

◹ k2tog   ☐ pattern repeat

Leg

Loosely CO 72 sts. Divide sts evenly on 4 dpn (18 sts per needle), place marker (pm), and join for working in the rnd, being careful not to twist sts. Knit 1 rnd. Purl 1 rnd. Work Rnds 1–6 of Lace chart 6 times.

Heel

Heel Flap

K18, turn work, sl 1, p35—36 heel sts centered over back of leg; rem 36 sts will be worked later for instep. Work 36 heel sts back and forth in rows as foll:

Row 1: (RS) *Sl 1 kwise with yarn in back (wyb), k1; rep from *.

Rows 2 and 4: (WS) Sl 1 pwise with yarn in front (wyf), p35.

Row 3: Sl 1 kwise wyb, *sl 1 kwise wyb, k1; rep from *, end k2.

Rep Rows 1–4 for a total of 40 rows—20 chain sts along each selvedge edge of heel flap.

Turn Heel

Work short-rows to shape heel as foll:

Row 1: (RS) *Sl 1 kwise wyb, k1; rep from * across 22 sts, ssk, turn work.

Row 2: (WS) Sl 1 pwise wyf, p8, p2tog, turn.

Row 3: Sl 1 kwise wyb, work 8 sts in established heel patt, ssk, turn.

Row 4: Sl 1 pwise wyf, p8, p2tog, turn.

Rep Rows 3 and 4, keeping in established patt, until all heel sts have been worked, ending with a WS row—10 sts rem.

Shape Gussets

Pick up sts along selvedge edges of heel flap and rejoin for working in the rnd as foll:

Rnd 1: On Needle 1, sl 1 pwise wyb, k9, pick up and knit 22 sts along right edge of heel flap; on Needle 2, work 18 sts according to Row 1 of chart as established; on Needle 3, work 18 sts according to Row 1 of chart as established; on Needle 4, pick up and knit 22 sts along left edge of heel flap then work first 5 heel sts from Needle 1 again— 90 sts total; 27 sts on Needle 1; 18 sts each on Needle 2 and Needle 3; 27 sts on Needle 4.

Rnd 2: On Needle 1, work to last 2 sts, k2tog; on Needle 2 and Needle 3, work as established; on Needle 4, ssk, work to end—2 sts dec'd.

Rep the last rnd 12 times more—64 sts rem; 14 sts each on Needle 1 and Needle 4, 18 sts each on Needle 2 and Needle 3.

Foot

Cont as established, working instep sts as charted and sole sts in St st, until a total of 14 patt reps have been worked from CO—piece should measure about 7" (18 cm) from back of heel.

Toe

Adjust sts by placing the first 2 sts from Needle 2 onto Needle 1 and the last 2 sts from Needle 3 onto Needle 4—16 sts on each needle.

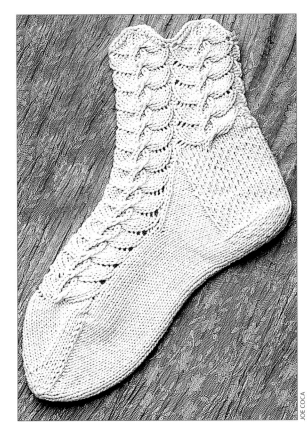

Rnd 1: On Needle 1, work to last 3 sts, k2tog, k1; on Needle 2, k1, ssk, work to end; on Needle 3, work to last 3 sts, k2tog, k1; on Needle 4, k1, ssk, work to end—4 sts dec'd.

Rnd 2: Work even.

Rep Rnds 1 and 2 until 32 sts rem (8 sts on each needle). Rep Rnd 1 (dec every rnd) until 8 sts rem (2 sts on each needle).

Finishing

Break yarn, thread tail through rem sts, pull snug to tighten, and fasten off. Weave in loose ends. Block lightly

from the Spring 2005 issue of *Interweave Knits*

CABLE RIB SOCKS

Erica Alexander

For Erica Alexander, handknitted socks top the list of life's little pleasures. The leg and instep of these socks are ribbed and decorated with a single classic cable at each side. Although Erica worked all the cable crosses in the same direction in the pair at left, these instructions are for working the cables as mirror images on each side of the foot.

FINISHED SIZE
About 7" (18 cm) foot circumference and 10" (25.5 cm) foot length. To fit a woman. *Note:* To make these socks larger or smaller, use needles one or two sizes larger or smaller and lengthen or shorten the foot as necessary.

YARN
Fingering-weight yarn (CYCA #1 Super Fine).
Shown here: Lana Grossa Meilenweit Cotton (45% cotton, 42% wool, 13% polyamide; 208 yd [190 m]/50 g): #47 green, 2 balls.

NEEDLES
Upper leg—size 2 (2.5 mm): set of 4 double-pointed (dpn). Lower leg and foot—size 1 (2.25 mm): set of 4 dpn. Adjust needle sizes if necessary to obtain the correct gauge.

NOTIONS
Markers (m); cable needle (cn); tapestry needle.

GAUGE
16 stitches and 24 rounds = 2" (5 cm) in stockinette stitch worked in the round on size 1 (2.25 mm) needles.

STITCH GUIDE
Cable Rib
Rnds 1–3: *K2, p1; rep from *.
Rnd 4: [K2, p1] 9 times, sl 3 sts onto cn and hold in front, k2, slip purl st from cn onto left needle and purl it, k2 from cn, p1, [k2, p1] 9 times, sl 3 sts onto cn and hold in back, k2, slip purl st from cn onto left needle and purl it, k2 from cn, p1.
Rnds 5–10: *K2, p1; rep from *.
Repeat Rnds 1–10 for pattern.

Instep Rib (worked over 34 sts)
Rnds 1–9: [P1, k2] 11 times, p1.
Rnd 10: P1, sl 3 sts onto cn and hold in front, k2, slip purl st from cn onto left needle and purl it, k2 from cn, [p1, k2] 7 times, p1, sl 3 sts onto cn and hold in back, k2, slip purl st from cn onto left needle and purl it, k2 from cn, p1.
Repeat Rnds 1–10 for pattern.

Leg

With size 2 (2.5 mm) needles, loosely CO 66 sts. Arrange sts evenly on 3 dpn, place marker (pm), and join for working in the rnd, being careful not to twist sts. Rep Rnds 1–10 of cable rib patt (see Stitch Guide) until piece measures 4" (10 cm) from CO. Change to size 1 (2.25 mm) needles and cont in patt as established until Rnd 4 of patt has been worked 10 times—94 rows of cable rib completed; piece measures about 8" (20.5 cm) from beg.

Heel

Heel Flap

Work 29 sts in patt, turn work around, sl 1 pwise with yarn in front (wyf), p31—32 heel sts centered over back of leg; rem 34 sts will be worked later for instep (the sts at each side of the instep should be the purl st from the center of each cable). Work 32 heel sts back and forth in rows as foll:

Row 1: (RS) *Sl 1 pwise with yarn in back (wyb), k1; rep from *.

Row 2: (WS) Sl 1 pwise wyf, purl to end.

Rep Rows 1 and 2 until a total of 32 rows have been worked, ending with a WS row—16 chain sts along each selvedge edge.

Turn Heel

Work short-rows to shape heel as foll:

Row 1: (RS) K18, ssk, k1, turn work.

Row 2: (WS) Sl 1 pwise wyf, p5, p2tog, p1, turn.

Row 3: Sl 1 pwise wyb, knit to 1 st before gap formed on previous row, ssk (1 st each side of gap), k1, turn.

Row 4: Sl 1 pwise wyf, purl to 1 st before gap formed on previous row, p2tog (1 st each side of gap), p1, turn.

Rep Rows 3 and 4 until all heel sts have been worked—18 sts rem.

Shape Gussets

Pick up sts along selvedge edges of heel flap and rejoin for working in the rnd as foll:

Rnd 1: With Needle 1, work 18 heel sts as sl 1, k17, then pick up and knit 18 sts along left side of heel flap; with Needle 2, work Rnd 1 of instep rib patt (see Stitch Guide) over 34 instep sts; with Needle 3, pick up and knit 18 sts along right side of heel flap, then knit the first 9 sts from Needle 1 again—88 sts total; 27 sts each on Needles 1 and 3; 34 instep sts on Needle 2. Rnd begins at center of heel.

Rnd 2: On Needle 1, knit to last 2 sts, k2tog; on Needle 2, cont in instep rib patt; on Needle 3, ssk, knit to end—2 sts dec'd.

Rnd 3: Work even in patt.

Rep Rnds 2 and 3 eleven more times—64 sts rem; 15 sts each on Needle 1 and Needle 3; 34 instep sts on Needle 2.

Foot

Cont even in patt (work instep patt on Needle 2; work St st on Needle 1 and Needle 3) until foot measures about 8" (20.5 cm) from back of heel, or 2" (5 cm) less than desired total length, ending with Rnd 2 of instep rib patt (2 rnds after last cable crossing rnd).

Toe

Knit 1 rnd, shifting the first st from Needle 2 onto Needle 1 and the last st from Needle 2 onto Needle 3—16 sts each on Needle 1 and Needle 3; 32 instep sts on Needle 2.

Rnd 1: On Needle 1, knit to last 2 sts, k2tog; on Needle 2, ssk, knit to last 2 sts, k2tog; on Needle 3, ssk, knit to end—4 sts dec'd.

Rnd 2: Knit.

Rep Rnds 1 and 2 seven more times— 32 sts rem; 8 sts each on Needle 1 and Needle 3; 16 sts on Needle 2. Rep Rnd 1 (dec *every* rnd) 4 times—16 sts rem; 4 sts each on Needle 1 and Needle 3; 8 sts on Needle 2. With Needle 3, knit sts from Needle 1—8 sts each on 2 needles.

Finishing

Cut yarn, leaving a 12" (30.5 cm) tail. Thread tail on a tapestry needle and use the Kitchener st (see Glossary, page 123) to graft sts tog. Weave in loose ends. Block lightly.

Diagonal Cross-Rib Socks

Ann Budd

For these handsome socks, Ann Budd used a diagonal cross pattern that is achieved by knitting a simple twist every other row. For mirror symmetry, the columns on one sock are knitted with a left-leaning stitch, while the other sock features a right-leaning stitch. The upper leg is worked on needles one size larger to accommodate the shape of the calf, a technique Ann borrowed from Pricilla Gibson-Roberts.

FINISHED SIZE
About 9" (23 cm) foot circumference and 10¼" (26 cm) foot length. To fit a man. *Note:* To make a woman's size, use needles one or two sizes smaller and shorten the foot as necessary.

YARN
Fingering-weight yarn (CYCA #1 Super Fine).
Shown here: Brown Sheep Wildfoote Luxury Sock Yarn (75% washable wool, 25% nylon; 215 yd [197 m]/50 g): #SY41 dark carmel (rust), 2 balls.

NEEDLES
Upper leg—size 3 (3.25 mm): set of 4 double-pointed (dpn). Lower leg and foot—size 2 (2.75 mm): set of 4 dpn. Adjust needle sizes if necessary to obtain the correct gauge.

NOTIONS
Marker (m); tapestry needle.

GAUGE
16 stitches and 19 rounds = 2" (5 cm) in stockinette stitch worked in the round on size 2 (2.75 mm) needles.

Leg

With size 3 (3.25 mm) needles and using the old Norwegian method (see Glossary, page 121), CO 70 sts. Arrange sts as evenly as possible on 3 dpn, place marker (pm), and join for working in the rnd, being careful not to twist sts.

Cuff

*K5, p2; rep from * to end. Rep the last rnd until piece measures 1" (2.5 cm) from CO.

Leg Pattern

Using Left Diagonal Cross Rib chart for first sock and Right Diagonal Cross Rib chart for second sock, rep Rnds 1–8 of chart until

piece measures about 3½" (9 cm) from CO, ending with Rnd 8 of patt. Change to size 2 (2.75 mm) needles and cont in patt from chart until piece measures about 8" (20.5 cm) from CO, ending with Rnd 8 of patt.

Heel

Heel Flap

K13, turn work around, sl 1 pwise with yarn in front (wyf), p33—34 heel sts approximately centered at back of leg; when viewed from RS, leg patt will be aligned over heel sts beg with k5 and ending with p1. Rem 36 sts will be worked later for instep. Work 34 heel sts back and forth in rows as foll:

Row 1: (RS) *Sl 1 kwise with yarn in back (wyb), k1; rep from * to end of row.

Row 2: (WS) Sl 1 pwise with wyf, purl to end.

Rep Rows 1 and 2 until a total of 34 rows have been worked—17 chain sts at each selvedge edge.

Turn Heel

Work short-rows to shape heel as foll:

Row 1: (RS) K19, ssk, k1, turn work.

Row 2: (WS) Sl 1 pwise wyf, p5, p2tog, p1, turn.

Row 3: Sl 1 kwise wyb, knit to 1 st before gap produced by previous row, ssk (1 st from each side of gap), k1, turn.

Row 4: Sl 1 pwise wyf, purl to 1 st before gap produced by previous row, p2tog (1 st from each side of gap), p1, turn.

Rep Rows 3 and 4 until all heel sts have been worked—20 heel sts rem.

☐ knit

• purl

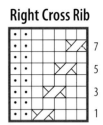 LT: Knit the second st on left needle through the back loop but do not slip sts from needle, knit the first 2 sts on left needle tog through their back loops, and slip both sts from needle

RT: Knit 2 sts together but do not slip sts from needle, knit the first st on left needle again, and slip both sts from needle

☐ pattern repeat

Left Cross Rib

Right Cross Rib

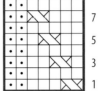

Shape Gussets

Pick up sts along selvedge edges of heel flap and rejoin for working in the rnd as foll:

Rnd 1: With Needle 1, k20 heel sts, then pick up and knit 18 sts, along edge of heel flap; with Needle 2, work across 36 instep sts in patt as established; with Needle 3, pick up and knit 18 sts along other edge of heel flap, then knit the first 10 heel sts from Needle 1 again—92 sts total; 28 sts each on Needle 1 and Needle 3; 36 instep sts on Needle 2. Slip last st on Needle 2 onto Needle 3—28 sts on Needle 1, 35 sts on Needle 2 (these sts beg and end with p1), 29 sts on Needle 3. Rnd begins at center of heel.

Rnd 2: On Needle 1, knit to last 3 sts, k2tog, k1; on Needle 2, work in patt as established; on Needle 3, k1, ssk, knit to end—2 sts dec'd.

Rnd 3: Cont in patt as established (work sts on Needle 2 in patt; work sts on Needle 1 and Needle 3 in St st).

Rep Rnds 2 and 3 until 70 sts rem.

Foot

Cont even in patt as established until piece measures about 7¾" (19.5 cm) from back of heel, or about 2½" (6.5 cm) less than desired total foot length, ending with Rnd 8 of patt.

Toe

Work in St st as foll:

Rnd 1: On Needle 1, knit to last 3 sts, k2tog, k1; on Needle 2, k1, ssk, knit to last 3 sts, k2tog, k1; on Needle 3, k1, ssk, knit to end—4 sts dec'd.

Rnd 2: Knit.

Rep Rnds 1 and 2 until 34 sts rem. Rep Rnd 1 *every* rnd until 14 sts rem. Knit the sts on Needle 2 onto the end of Needle 3—7 sts each on 2 needles.

Finishing

Cut yarn, leaving a 12" (30.5 cm) tail. Thread tail on a tapestry needle and use the Kitchener st (see Glossary, page 123) to join sts. Weave in loose ends. Block lightly.

from the September/October 2003 issue of *PieceWork*

JOE COCA

ANNIVERSARY SOCKS

Nancy Bush

Although readers of *Knits* know and love Nancy Bush's sock patterns, they

probably haven't seen these delightful "party socks." Nancy is the treasured

knitting contributor to *PieceWork*, an Interweave publication dedicated to

a variety of traditional needle arts. These socks, which she designed to

commemorate *PieceWork's* tenth anniversary, were inspired by a number of

historic socks she'd seen in various museums over the course of a decade.

In the style of nineteenth-century European women's stockings, only the

front of the socks is decorated to show beneath a long skirt.

FINISHED SIZE

About 7½" (19 cm) foot circumference and 9½" (24 cm) foot
length. To fit a woman. *Note:* To make the socks larger or smaller,
use needles one or two sizes larger or smaller and lengthen or
shorten the foot as necessary.

YARN

Fingering-weight yarn (CYCA #1 Super Fine).
Shown here: Knit One Crochet Too Richesse et Soie (65%
cashmere, 35% silk; 145 yd [133 m]/25 g): #9521 moss,
3 skeins. *Note:* This yarn has been discontinued; substitute
the fingering-weight luxury yarn of your choice.

NEEDLES

Size 1 (2.5 mm): set of 5 double-pointed (dpn). Adjust needle
size if necessary to obtain the correct gauge.

NOTIONS

Marker (m); tapestry needle.

GAUGE

18 stitches and 24 rounds = 2" (5 cm) in stockinette stitch
worked in the round.

STITCH GUIDE

Left Cross (LC2) (worked over 2 stitches)
Knit into the back of the second st on left needle, knit into the
front of the first st, then slip both sts off the needle.

Leg

Holding 2 needles tog, CO 65 sts. Remove second needle carefully and arrange sts on 4 dpn so that there are 16 sts on Needle 1, 15 sts on Needle 2, and 17 sts each on Needle 3 and Needle 4. Join for working in the rnd, being careful not to twist sts. Purl 1 rnd. Work lace diamond patt as foll:

Rnds 1 and 2: P1, *k2, p1, k1, p1; rep from * to last 4 sts, k2, p1, k1.

Rnd 3: P1, *LC2 (see Stitch Guide), p1, k1, p1; rep from * to last 4 sts, LC2, p1, k1.

Rnds 4, 5, and 6: P1, *k2, p1, k1, p1; rep from * to last 4 sts, k2, p1, k1.

Rnd 7: P1, *LC2, p1, k1, p1; rep from * to last 4 sts, LC2, p1, k1.

Rep Rnds 4–7 three more times. *Next rnd:* P16, *k2, p3; rep from * 6 times, k2, p15, p2tog—64 sts rem. Arrange sts so that there are 16 sts each on Needle 1 and Needle 4, 13 instep sts on Needle 2, and 19 instep sts on Needle 3. Rnd begins at back of leg. Work in patt as foll:

Rnds 1, 2, 4, 6, 8, and 10: K16, *k2, p1, k6, p1; rep from * 2 more times, k2, k16.

Rnds 3 and 11: K16, *LC2, p1, k2, yo, k2tog, k2, p1; rep from * 2 more times, LC2, k16.

Rnds 5 and 9: K16, *LC2, p1, k1, yo, k2tog, yo, k2tog, k1, p1; rep from * 2 more times, LC2, k16.

Rnd 7: K16, *LC2, p1, [yo, k2tog] 3 times, p1; rep from * 2 more times, LC2, k16.

Rnd 12: Rep Rnd 1.

Rep Rnds 1–12 until leg measures 9" (23 cm) or desired length to heel, ending with Needle 3 (ready to work last 16 sts of rnd).

Heel
Heel Flap

The 32 sts on Needle 4 and Needle 1 form the heel flap; rem 32 sts will be worked later for instep. Beg with first st on Needle 4, work heel sts back and forth in rows as foll:

Row 1: (RS) *Sl 1 kwise with yarn in back (wyb), k1; rep from * across 32 sts (the sts on Needle 4 and Needle 1).

Row 2: (WS) Sl 1 pwise with yarn in front (wyf), p31.

Row 3: Sl 1 kwise wyb, *sl 1 kwise wyb, k1; rep from * to last 2 sts, k2.

Row 4: Sl 1 pwise wyf, p31.

Rep Rows 1–4 until a total of 32 rows have been worked, ending with a WS row— 16 chain sts along each selvedge edge.

Turn Heel

Work short-rows to shape heel as foll:

Row 1: (RS) K18, ssk, k1.

Row 2: (WS) Sl 1 pwise wyf, p5, p2tog, p1.

Row 3: Sl 1 kwise wyb, knit to 1 st from gap formed on previous row, ssk (1 st each side of gap), k1.

Row 4: Sl 1 pwise wyf, purl to 1 st from gap formed on previous row, p2tog (1 st each side of gap), p1.

Rep Rows 3 and 4 until all heel sts have been worked—18 heel sts rem.

Shape Gussets

Pick up sts along selvedge edges of heel flap and rejoin for working in the rnd as foll:

Rnd 1: K18 heel sts, pick up and knit 16 sts along right side of heel flap, k32 instep sts in patt as established, pick up and knit 16 sts along left side of heel flap, then knit the first 9 heel sts again—82 sts total. Arrange sts so that there are 25 sts each on Needle 1 and Needle 4, 13 instep sts on Needle 2, and 19 instep sts on Needle 3. Rnd begins at center of heel.

Rnd 2: On Needle 1, knit to last 3 sts, k2tog, k1; on Needle 2 and Needle 3, work patt as established; on Needle 4, k1, ssk, knit to end—2 sts dec'd.

Rnd 3: Work even in patt (knit sts on Needle 1 and Needle 4; work instep sts as established).

Rep Rnds 2 and 3 until 64 sts rem—16 sts each on Needle 1 and Needle 4. Cont in patt as established until a total of 12 lace diamond patt reps have been worked, and *at the same time*, on the last rnd, k2tog the last 2 sts on Needle 3, work to end of rnd—63 sts rem.

Foot

Cont instep sts in patt and sole sts in St st as established until piece measures 8" (20.5 cm) from back of heel, or about 1½" (3.8 cm) less than desired total foot length.

Toe

Arrange sts evenly onto 3 needles (21 sts each needle), keeping beg of rnd at center of sole.

Rnd 1: *K1, ssk, knit to last 3 sts on Needle 1, k2tog, k1; rep from * on each needle—6 sts dec'd.

Rnd 2: Knit.

Rep Rnds 1 and 2 until 15 sts rem (5 sts on each needle). *Next rnd:* *K1, sl 1, k1, psso, k1; rep from * on each needle—9 sts rem.

Finishing

Cut yarn, thread tail through rem sts, pull snug to tighten, and fasten off. Weave in loose ends. Block lightly.

from the Spring 2005 issue of *Interweave Knits*

Go With the Flow Socks

Evelyn A. Clark

A pair of warm, pretty socks is an undeniable pleasure. In a soft, luxurious merino, this pair would make a great gift for a friend, or yourself! The short cuff is worked in a lace ladder pattern, and a simple combination of vertical stitch patterns runs from the cuff to the toe. The stitch patterns repeat every four rounds, so they're easy to memorize and simple to knit.

FINISHED SIZE
About 6" (15 cm) foot circumference, relaxed, and about 9½" (24 cm) foot length. To fit a woman. *Note:* To make the socks larger or smaller, use needles one or two sizes larger or smaller and lengthen or shorten the foot as necessary.

YARN
Fingering-weight yarn (CYCA #1 Super Fine).
Shown here: Cherry Tree Hill Supersock Solids (100% merino; 370 yd [338 m]/4 oz): Nantucket red, 1 skein.

NEEDLES
Size 1 (2.25 mm): set of 4 double-pointed (dpn). Adjust needle size if necessary to obtain the correct gauge.

NOTIONS
Marker (m); tapestry needle.

GAUGE
18 stitches and 26 rounds = 2" (5 cm) in stockinette stitch worked in the round.

NOTE
Because this lace pattern has a lot of stretch, it is important to try on the sock or to stretch it widthwise when measuring the length.

Cuff

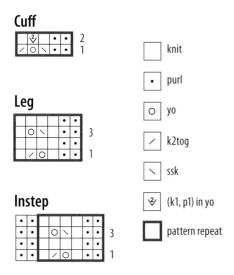

Leg

Instep

Legend:

- knit
- • purl
- o yo
- / k2tog
- \ ssk
- (k1, p1) in yo
- pattern repeat

Leg

Loosely CO 60 sts. Arrange sts on 3 dpn so that there are 18 sts each on Needle 1 and Needle 2, and 24 sts on Needle 3. Place marker (pm) and join for working in the rnd, being careful not to twist sts. Purl 1 rnd. Work Rnds 1–2 of Cuff chart 5 times, then purl 1 rnd—piece should measure about 1" (2.5 cm) from beg. Work Rnds 1–4 of Leg chart 20 times—piece should measure about 7¼" (18.5 cm) from CO.

Heel

Heel Flap

K14, turn work around, sl 1 pwise with yarn in front (wyf), p27—28 heel sts centered at back of leg; rem 32 sts will be worked later for instep. Work 28 heel sts back and forth in rows as foll:

Row 1: (RS) *Sl 1 kwise with yarn in back (wyb), k1; rep from * to end of row.

Row 2: (WS) Sl 1 pwise wyf, purl to end.

Rep Rows 1 and 2 a total of 18 times, then work Row 1 once more—18 chain sts at each selvedge edge; heel flap measures about 2" (5 cm) long.

Turn Heel

Work short-rows to shape heel as foll:

Row 1: (WS) Sl 1 pwise wyf, p14, p2tog, p1, turn work.

Row 2: (RS) Sl 1 pwise wyb, k3, ssk, k1, turn.

Row 3: Sl 1, purl to 1 st before gap formed on previous row, p2tog (1 st each side of gap), p1, turn.

Row 4: Sl 1, knit to 1 st before gap formed on previous row, ssk (1 st each side of gap), k1, turn.

Rep Rows 3 and 4 until all heel sts have been worked—16 heel sts rem.

Shape Gussets

Pick up sts along selvedge edges of heel flap and rejoin for working in the rnd as foll:

Rnd 1: With Needle 1 (needle holding heel sts), pick up and knit 19 sts along left edge of heel flap; with Needle 2, work 32 instep sts according to Rnd 1 of Instep chart; with Needle 3, pick up and knit 19 sts along right edge of heel flap, then knit the first 8 heel sts from Needle 1 again—86 sts total; 27 sts each on Needle 1 and Needle 3; 32 instep sts on Needle 2. Rnd begins at center of heel.

Rnd 2: On Needle 1, k8, [k1 through back loop (tbl)] 19 times; on Needle 2, cont in instep patt as established; on Needle 3, [k1tbl] 19 times, k8.

Rnd 3: On Needle 1, knit to last 2 sts, k2tog;

on Needle 2, cont in instep patt as established; on Needle 3, ssk, knit to end—2 sts dec'd.

Rnd 4: On Needle 1, knit; on Needle 2, work instep patt as established; on Needle 3, knit.

Rep Rnds 3 and 4 until 60 sts rem—14 sts each on Needle 1 and Needle 3; 32 instep sts on Needle 2.

Foot

Cont even (work sts on Needle 2 in instep patt as established; work sts on Needle 1 and Needle 3 in St st) until foot measures 8" (20.5 cm) from back of heel, or about 1½" (3.8 cm) less than desired total foot length (measured with sock on foot or with lace pattern stretched horizontally; see Note), ending with an even-numbered rnd of instep patt.

JOE COCA

Toe

Knit 1 rnd, redistributing sts as foll: On Needle 1, k14, k1 from Needle 2; on Needle 2, k30; on Needle 3, knit last st from Needle 2, then k14—15 sts each on Needle 1 and Needle 3; 30 sts on Needle 2.

Rnd 1: On Needle 1, knit to last 3 sts, k2tog, k1; on Needle 2, k1, ssk, knit to last 3 sts, k2tog, k1; on Needle 3, k1, ssk, knit to end—4 sts dec'd.

Rnd 2: Knit.

Rep Rnds 1 and 2 until 32 sts rem, then work Rnd 1 *only* until 12 sts rem. Knit 3 sts from Needle 1 onto Needle 3—6 sts each on 2 needles.

Finishing

Cut yarn, leaving a 12" (30.5 cm) tail. With tail threaded on a tapestry needle, use the Kitchener st (see Glossary, page 123) to join sts. Weave in loose ends. Block lightly.

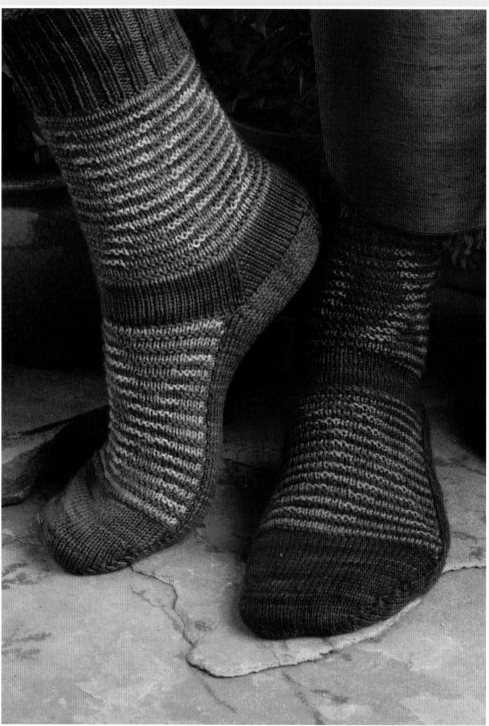

from the Summer 2002 issue of *Interweave Knits*

Hidden Passion Socks

Jaya Srikrishnan

Depending on the light or angle of view, Jaya Srikrishnan's illusion socks reveal colorful stripes or "hugs and kisses." The foot is worked flat as a strip that extends along the instep from the ankle to the short-row toe, then it continues along the sole to the heel, and is joined to the instep along the way. The heel is shaped with a standard gusset worked upside down.

FINISHED SIZE
7 (8½, 10)" (18 [21.5, 25.5] cm) foot circumference and 8¾ (9½, 10¼)" (22 [24, 26] cm) foot length. To fit adult small (medium, large).

YARN
Fingering-weight yarn (CYCA #1 Super Fine).
Shown here: Lorna's Laces Shepherd Sock (80% superwash wool, 20% nylon; 215 yd [195 m]/ 50 g): Color A, 1 (2, 2) skein(s); color B, 1 skein. Shown in #2ns Manzanita (A) with #9ns pewter (B), and #43ns sage (A) with #7ns cedar (B).

NEEDLES
Size 0 (2.0 mm): set of 4 double-pointed (dpn). One needle two or more sizes larger for binding off (optional). Adjust needle size if necessary to obtain the correct gauge.

NOTIONS
Markers (m); tapestry needle.

GAUGE
18 stitches and 28 rows = 2" (5 cm) in stockinette stitch.

STITCH GUIDE
RS join (worked on RS rows)
Sl the last st pwise with yarn in front (wyf) to right needle, use left needle to pick up the 2 loops of the edge st on the adjoining strip, sl the last st back onto left needle and purl this st tog with the 2 loops, turn, sl first st kwise with yarn in back (wyb), purl to end of row.

WS join (worked on WS rows)
Sl the last st kwise wyb to right needle, use left needle to pick up the 2 loops of the edge st on the adjoining strip, knit this st, pass slipped st over it, turn, sl the first st pwise wyf, knit to end of row.

NOTES
- Begin and end all rows (when working back and forth) with a chain selvedge as foll: K1tbl (through back loop) at beg of each row; sl 1 pwise wyf (with yarn in front) at the end of each row. This is not indicated on the chart.
- When changing colors, pick up the new color from *under* the old to prevent holes when working in the round and to give a smooth chain selvedge when working in rows.

Foot

With A and using the knitted method (see Glossary, page 120), CO 32 (38, 44) sts. Join B. Beg and end as specified for your size, work Rows 1–78 of Hugs and Kisses chart across all sts for top of foot, always picking up the new color from *under* the old (see Notes)—piece measures about 5½" (14 cm). Cut off B. With A only, work St st for ¾ (1, 1)" (2 [2.5, 2.5] cm). To adjust foot length, work more or fewer rows in St st here.

Toe

Work short-rows (see Glossary, page 125) to shape toe as foll:

Row 1: Knit.

Row 2: Sl 1, purl to last st, wrap last st, turn.

Row 3: Sl 1, knit to last st, wrap last st, turn.

Row 4: Sl 1, purl to 1 st before wrapped st, wrap next st, turn.

Row 5: Sl 1, knit to 1 st before wrapped st, wrap next st, turn.

Rep Rows 4 and 5 until 8 (10, 11) sts have been wrapped on each side—16 (18, 22) sts rem unwrapped in center. *Next row:* (WS) Sl 1, purl to wrapped st, purl next st tog with wrap, turn. *Next row:* (RS) Sl 1, knit to wrapped st, knit next st tog with wrap through the back loop, turn. Rep the last 2 rows until all wrapped sts have been worked—32 (38, 44) unwrapped sts.

Sole

Working back and forth in rows in St st with A, join sole to the top-of-foot sts using the RS join on each knit row and the WS join on each purl row (see Stitch Guide).

Cont working sole and join to sides of the charted design on top of foot until the sole reaches the CO row on top of foot.

Heel

Heel Flap

(Worked across 32 [38, 44] sts of sole) Working back and forth in rows with A, rep Rnds 1–4 of Heel chart for a total of 32 (38, 44) rows.

Turn Heel

Work 32 [38, 44] heel sts in short-rows as foll:

Row 1: (RS) Sl 1 pwise wyb, work 20 (24, 29) sts as established, ssk, turn—9 (11, 12) sts unworked at end of row.

Row 2: (WS) Sl 1 pwise wyf, p10 (12, 16), p2tog, turn—9 (11, 12) sts unworked at other side.

Row 3: Sl 1 pwise wyb, work 10 (12, 16) sts as established, ssk, turn.

Rep Rows 2 and 3 until all the sts from the sides have been incorporated into the heel—12 (14, 18) sts rem.

Shape Gussets

Pick up sts along selvedge edges of heel flap and rejoin for working in the rnd as foll:

Rnd 1: With Needle 1, k12 (14, 18) heel sts, then pick up and knit 16 (19, 22) sts along edge of heel flap; with Needle 2, pick up and knit 32 (38, 44) sts along CO row at top of foot for instep; with Needle 3, pick up and knit 16 (19, 22) sts along other edge of heel flap, then knit across the first 6 (7, 9) heel sts from Needle 1 again—76 (90, 106) sts total; 22 (26, 31) sts on Needle 1; 32 (38, 44) instep sts on Needle 2; 22 (26, 31) sts on Needle 3. Rnd begins at center of heel.

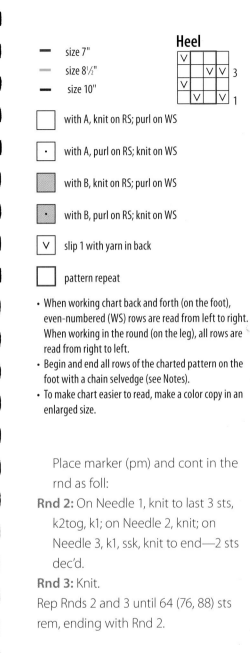

— size 7"

— size 8½"

— size 10"

Heel

□ with A, knit on RS; purl on WS

· with A, purl on RS; knit on WS

▨ with B, knit on RS; purl on WS

▨ with B, purl on RS; knit on WS

V slip 1 with yarn in back

□ pattern repeat

- When working chart back and forth (on the foot), even-numbered (WS) rows are read from left to right. When working in the round (on the leg), all rows are read from right to left.
- Begin and end all rows of the charted pattern on the foot with a chain selvedge (see Notes).
- To make chart easier to read, make a color copy in an enlarged size.

Place marker (pm) and cont in the rnd as foll:

Rnd 2: On Needle 1, knit to last 3 sts, k2tog, k1; on Needle 2, knit; on Needle 3, k1, ssk, knit to end—2 sts dec'd.

Rnd 3: Knit.

Rep Rnds 2 and 3 until 64 (76, 88) sts rem, ending with Rnd 2.

Leg

Join B. Beg and end as specified for your size, work Rows 1–78 of Hugs and Kisses chart across first 32 (38, 44) sts, then again on the next 32 (38, 44) sts so that the design completely encircles the leg. Cut off B.

Hugs and Kisses

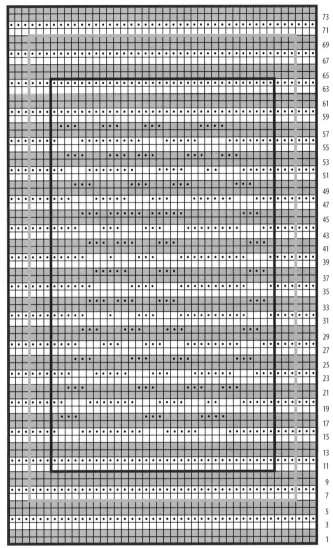

Cuff

With A, knit 0 (1, 1) rnd even. *Next rnd:* *K2, p2; rep from * to end of rnd. Cont in rib as established for 2½" (6.5 cm). Using larger needle, BO all sts extremely loosely.

Finishing

Weave in loose ends. Block lightly.

UNDULATING RIB SOCKS

Ann Budd

Inspired by a stitch pattern found in a Japanese knitting book, these socks feature an easily memorized pattern that alternates increases and decreases to create columns that widen and narrow. The pattern flows along the instep to create a somewhat elastic pattern that gently hugs the leg and foot. Depending on the yarn you choose, the resulting sock is appropriate for a man or woman.

FINISHED SIZE
About 7¼ (8½)" (18.5 [21.5] cm) foot circumference and 8½ (10)" (21.5 [25.5] cm) foot length. To fit a woman (man). *Note:* To make the socks larger or smaller, use needles one or two sizes larger or smaller and lengthen or shorten the foot as necessary.

YARN
Fingering-weight yarn (CYCA #1 Super Fine).
Shown here: Schoeller & Stahl Fortissima Colori (75% wool, 25% nylon; 229 yd [210 m]/50 g): #2412 brown/green/copper stripe, 2 balls.

NEEDLES
Upper leg—size 4 (3.5 mm): set of 4 double-pointed (dpn). Lower leg and foot—size 3 (3.25 mm): set of 4 dpn. Adjust needle sizes if necessary to obtain the correct gauge.

NOTIONS
Marker (m); tapestry needle.

GAUGE
18 stitches and 24 rounds = 2" (5 cm) in stockinette stitch worked in the round on size 3 (3.25 mm) needles.

Leg

With size 4 (3.5 mm) needles, loosely CO 66 (78) sts. Arrange sts as evenly as possible on 3 dpn, place marker (pm), and join for working in the rnd, being careful not to twist sts. Rnd begins at back of leg. *Next rnd:* *K3, p1, k1, p1; rep from * to end. Rep the last rnd 9 more times—10 rnds total; piece measures about 1" (2.5 cm) from CO. Change to Undulating Rib chart and rep Rnds 1–16 of chart until piece measures about 3½ (4)" (9 [10] cm) from CO. Change to size 3 (3.25 mm) needles and cont in patt from chart until piece measures about 7 (8)" (18 [20.5] cm) from CO, or desired length to heel, ending with Rnd 1 of chart.

Heel

Heel Flap

K17 (23), turn work around so WS is facing, sl 1, p31 (37)—32 (38) heel sts centered at back of leg (when viewed from RS, these sts beg with p1 and end with k1). Rem 34 (40) sts will be worked later for instep. Work 32 (38) heel sts back and forth in rows as foll:

Row 1: (RS) *Sl 1 kwise with yarn in back (wyb), k1; rep from * to end of row.

Row 2: (WS) Sl 1 pwise with yarn in front (wyf), purl to end.

Rep Rows 1 and 2 until a total of 32 (38) rows have been worked—16 (19) chain sts at each selvedge edge.

Turn Heel

Work short-rows to shape heel as foll:

Row 1: (RS) K18 (21), ssk, k1, turn work.

Row 2: (WS) Sl 1 pwise wyf, p5, p2tog, p1, turn.

Row 3: Sl 1 pwise wyb, knit to 1 st before gap formed on previous row, ssk (1 st from each side of gap), k1, turn.

Row 4: Sl 1 pwise wyf, purl to 1 st before gap formed on previous row, p2tog (1 st from each side of gap), p1, turn.

Rep Rows 3 and 4 until all heel sts have been worked—18 (22) heel sts rem.

Shape Gussets

Pick up sts along selvedge edges of heel flap and rejoin for working in the rnd as foll:

Rnd 1: With Needle 1, k18 (22) heel sts, then pick up and knit 17 (19) sts along edge of heel flap; with Needle 2, work across 34 (40) instep sts in patt as charted; with Needle 3, pick up and knit 17 (19) sts along other edge of heel flap, then knit the first 9 (11) heel sts from Needle 1 again—86 (100) sts total; 26 (30) sts each on Needle 1 and Needle 3; 34 (40) instep sts on Needle 2. Slip first st

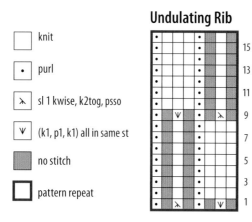

Undulating Rib

knit

· purl

⋋ sl 1 kwise, k2tog, psso

Ⅴ (k1, p1, k1) all in same st

no stitch

pattern repeat

on Needle 3 back onto Needle 2—
26 (30) sts on Needle 1; 35 (41) sts
on Needle 2 (these sts now begin
and end with p1), 25 (29) sts on
Needle 3. Rnd begins at center
of heel.

Rnd 2: On Needle 1, knit to last 3
sts, k2tog, k1; on Needle 2, work in
patt as established; on Needle 3, k1,
ssk, knit to end—2 sts dec'd.

Rnd 3: Cont in patt as established
(work sts on Needle 2 in patt from
chart; work sts on Needle 1 and
Needle 3 in St st).

Rep Rnds 2 and 3 until 66 (78) sts rem.

Foot

Cont even in patt as established
until piece measures about 6¾ (8)"
(17 [20.5] cm) from back of heel, or about
1¾ (2)" (4.5 [5] cm) less than desired total
foot length.

Toe

Work in St st as foll:

Rnd 1: On Needle 1, knit to last 2 sts,
k2tog; on Needle 2, p1, ssk, knit to last
3 sts, k2tog, p1; on Needle 3, ssk, knit to
end—4 sts dec'd.

Rnd 2: Work even as established (knit the
knits and purl the purls).

Rep Rnds 1 and 2 until 34 (38) sts rem. Rep
Rnd 1 *every* rnd until 14 sts rem. Knit the
sts on Needle 1 onto the end of Needle
3—7 sts each on 2 needles.

Finishing

Cut yarn, leaving a 12" (30.5 cm) tail. Thread
tail on a tapestry needle and use the Kitchener st (see Glossary, page 123) to join sts.
Weave in loose ends. Block lightly.

JOE COCA

from the Winter 1997 issue of *Interweave Knits*

JOE COCA

EESTI TRAIL HIKING SOCKS

Nancy Bush

These men's hiking socks were modeled after a pair of socks Nancy Bush purchased in a village market in Kuressaare, on the island of Saaremaa in Estonia. She chose to substitute the snowflake or cross pattern for the heavy XO design of the original socks. Easy to knit, these socks make a perfect gift—or a project for any man who has discovered the pleasures of making handknit socks for himself.

FINISHED SIZE
About 9½" (24 cm) foot circumference and 10¾" (27.5 cm) foot length. To fit a man. *Note:* To make a woman's size, use needles one size smaller and shorten the foot as necessary.

YARN
Worsted-weight yarn (CYCA #4 Medium).
Shown here: Patons Rustic Wool (100% wool; 205 yd [187 m]/100 g): #1009 Natural (MC), 2 balls; #1008 Copper (CC), 1 ball. *Note:* This yarn has been discontinued; substitute the worsted-weight yarn of your choice.

NEEDLES
Size 3 (3.25 mm): set of 4 double-pointed (dpn). Adjust needle size if necessary to obtain the correct gauge.

NOTIONS
Marker (m); thread for reinforcing the heel and toe (optional); tapestry needle.

GAUGE
12 stitches and 15 rounds = 2" (5 cm) in stockinette stitch worked in the round, before blocking.

Leg

With MC, loosely CO 56 sts. Arrange sts as evenly as possible on 3 dpn, place marker (pm), and join for working in the rnd, being careful not to twist sts. Work k2, p2 ribbing for 21 rnds. Keeping in rib as established, work 2 rnds with C, 2 rnds with MC, 1 rnd with C, 1 rnd with MC, 1 rnd with C, 2 rnds with MC, 2 rnds with CC, and 13 rnds with MC. With MC, work 5 rnds St st. Work Rnds 1–21 of Star chart, inc and dec 8 sts evenly spaced on Rnds 4 and 19 as indicated. With MC, work St st for 9 rnds, or until piece measures desired length to heel.

Heel

Join reinforcing thread if desired.

Heel Flap

K14, turn work around. Sl 1 pwise with yarn in front (wyf), p27—28 heel sts centered over back of leg; rem 28 sts will be worked later for the instep. Work 28 heel sts back and forth in rows as foll:

Row 1: (RS) *Sl 1 kwise with yarn in back (wyb), k1; rep from *.

Row 2: (WS) Sl 1 pwise wyf, purl to end.

Work these 2 rows 14 times total, ending with a WS row—14 chain sts along each selvedge edge.

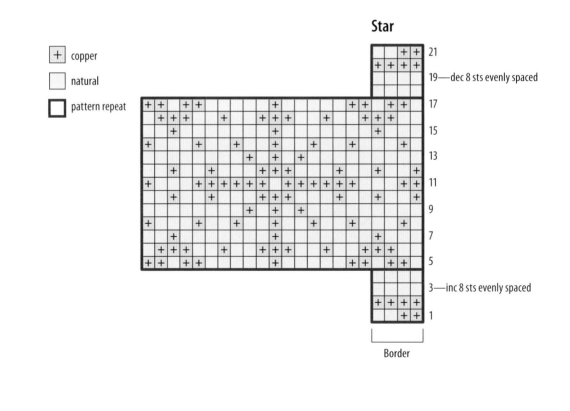

Star

+ copper

natural

pattern repeat

21
19—dec 8 sts evenly spaced
17
15
13
11
9
7
5
3—inc 8 sts evenly spaced
1

Border

Turn Heel

Work short-rows to shape heel as foll:

Row 1: (RS) K16, ssk, k1, turn.

Row 2: (WS) Sl 1 pwise wyf, p5, p2tog, p1, turn.

Row 3: Sl 1 pwise wyb, knit to 1 st before gap formed on previous row, ssk (1 st each side of gap), k1, turn.

Row 4: Sl 1 pwise wyf, purl to 1 st before gap formed on previous row, p2tog (1 st each side of gap), p1, turn.

Rep Rows 3 and 4 until all heel sts have been worked, ending with a WS row—16 heel sts rem. On next row, k8. (Break off reinforcing thread, if it was used.)

Shape Gussets

Pick up sts along selvedge edges of heel flap and rejoin for working in the rnd as foll:

Rnd 1: With Needle 1, k8 rem heel sts, pick up and knit 14 sts along left edge of heel flap; with Needle 2, pick up and knit 1 st at base of heel flap, k28 instep sts, pick up and knit 1 st at base of other side of heel flap (these 2 extra sts will be dec'd on the next rnd; they help close up the hole that appears at the corner of instep and heel flap); with Needle 3, pick up and knit 14 sts along right edge of heel flap, k8 heel sts—74 sts total; 22 sts each on Needle 1 and Needle 3; 30 sts on Needle 2. Rnd begins at center of heel.

Rnd 2: On Needle 1, knit to last 3 sts, k2tog, k1; on Needle 2, k2tog, knit to last 2 sts, ssk; on Needle 3, k1, ssk, knit to end—2 sts dec'd.

Rnd 3: Knit.

Rep Rnds 2 and 3 until 56 sts rem.

Foot

Cont even in St st until foot measures about 3½" (9 cm) less than desired total length from heel to toe.

Toe

Join reinforcing thread if desired.

Rnd 1: *K6, k2tog; rep from *—49 sts rem.

Rnds 2–7: Knit.

Rnd 8: *K5, k2tog; rep from *—42 sts rem.

Rnds 9–13: Knit.

Rnd 14: *K4, k2tog; rep from *—35 sts rem.

Rnds 15–18: Knit.

Cont in this manner, working 1 fewer st bet each dec and knitting 1 fewer rnd bet dec rnds until 14 sts rem, ending with knit 1 rnd. *Next rnd:* *k2tog; rep from *—7 sts rem.

Finishing

Break yarn, leaving 8" (20.5 cm) tail. Thread tail on tapestry needle, draw through rem sts, pull snug to tighten, and fasten off. Weave in loose ends. Block lightly.

LACE-CUFF ANKLETS

Ann Budd

Linen might sound like an unusual choice for a sock, but this merino/linen blend brings out the best in both fibers. The softness, stretch, and memory of the fine wool create a comfortable sock that holds its shape. With a simple openwork ribbed cuff, these anklets are perfect summer socks. Begin the cuff on the largest-size needle, then switch to the medium size at the halfway point to allow the lace trim to fold over, then work the heel, foot, and toe with the smallest size. Finish off the lace cuff with a crocheted picot edge.

FINISHED SIZE
About 6¾ (8½)" (17 [21.5] cm) foot circumference and 7 (9½)" (18 [24] cm) foot length. To fit a child (woman). *Note:* To make the socks larger or smaller, use needles one or two sizes larger or smaller and lengthen or shorten the foot as necessary.

YARN
Sportweight yarn (CYCA #2 Fine).
Shown here: Louet Sales MerLin Tristan (40% merino, 60% linen; 250 yd [229 m]/100 g): #60 sage, 1 (2) skein(s).

NEEDLES
Lace cuff—sizes 4 and 3 (3.5 and 3.25 mm): set of 4 double-pointed (dpn). Foot—size 2 (3 mm): set of 4 dpn. Adjust needle sizes if necessary to obtain the correct gauge.

NOTIONS
Marker (m); tapestry needle; size F/5 (3.75 mm) crochet hook.

GAUGE
13 stitches and 19 rounds = 2" (5 cm) in stockinette stitch worked in the round on size 2 (3 mm) needles.

STITCH GUIDE
2 × 2 Openwork Rib (multiple of 4 sts)
Rnd 1: *K2, yo, ssk; rep from *.
Rnd 2: *K2tog, yo, k2; rep from *.
Repeat Rnds 1 and 2 for pattern.

JOE COCA

Cuff

Holding two size 4 (3.5 mm) needles tog, loosly CO 44 (56) sts. Carefully remove second needle from CO, arrange sts as evenly as possible on 3 dpn, place marker (pm), and join for working in the rnd, being careful not to twist sts. Knit 1 rnd. Work 2 × 2 openwork rib (see Stitch Guide) for a total of 10 (12) rnds. Change to size 3 (3.25 mm) needles and cont as established for 10 (12) more rnds—piece measures about 2½ (3)" (6.5 [7.5] cm) from CO. Change to size 2 (3 mm) needles and purl 1 rnd for cuff fold line. Bring yarn to front between needles, slip first st of next rnd as if to purl, wrap this st by bringing yarn to back between needles and return slipped st to left needle. Turn cuff inside out so that WS of lace pattern is outward. RS of remainder of sock will correspond to WS of lace patt so that the RS of lace will show on the outside of the sock when the cuff is folded down. Rnd begins at back of leg. *Next rnd:* *K1, p1; rep from * to end. Rep the last rnd until piece measures 2½ (3)" (6.5 [7.5] cm) from purled fold line. The ribbing will help hold the sock up and will be concealed by the lace section when the cuff is folded down.

Leg

Change to St st and knit 7 (9) rnds.

Heel

Heel Flap

K11 (14), turn work so WS is facing, sl 1 pwise with yarn in front (wyf), p21 (27)—22 (28) heel sts centered at back of leg; rem 22 (28) sts will be worked later for instep. Work 22 (28) heel sts back and forth in rows as foll:

Row 1: (RS) *Sl 1 kwise with yarn in back (wyb), k1; rep from * to end of row.

Row 2: (WS) Sl 1 pwise wyf, purl to end.

Rep Rows 1 and 2 until a total of 22 (28) rows have been worked—11 (14) chain sts at each selvedge edge.

Turn Heel

Work short-rows to shape heel as foll:

Row 1: (RS) K13 (16), ssk, k1, turn work.

Row 2: (WS) Sl 1, p5, p2tog, p1, turn.

Row 3: Sl 1, knit to 1 st before gap formed on previous row, ssk (1 st from each side of gap), k1, turn.

Row 4: Sl 1, purl to 1 st before gap formed on previous row, p2tog (1 st from each side of gap), p1, turn.

Rep Rows 3 and 4 until all heel sts have been worked—14 (16) heel sts rem.

Shape Gussets

Pick up sts along selvedge edges of heel flap and rejoin for working in the rnd as foll:

Rnd 1: With Needle 1, k14 (16) heel sts, then pick up and knit 12 (15) sts along edge of heel flap; with Needle 2, k22 (28) instep sts; with Needle 3, pick up and knit 12 (15) sts along other edge of heel flap, then knit the first 7 (8) heel sts from Needle 1 again—60 (74) sts total; 19 (23) sts each on Needle 1 and Needle 3, 22 (28) instep sts on Needle 2. Rnd begins at center of heel.

Rnd 2: On Needle 1, knit to last 3 sts, k2tog, k1; on Needle 2, knit; on Needle 3, k1, ssk, knit to end—2 sts dec'd.

Rnd 3: Knit.

Rep Rnds 2 and 3 until—44 (56) sts rem.

Foot

Cont even in St st until piece measures 5½ (7½)" (14.5 [19] cm) from back of heel, or about 1¼ (2)" (3.2 [5] cm) less than desired total foot length. Rearrange sts if necessary so that 11 (14) sole sts are on Needle 1, 22 (28) instep sts are on Needle 2, and rem 11 (14) sole sts are on Needle 3.

Toe

Rnd 1: On Needle 1, knit to last 3 sts, k2tog, k1; on Needle 2, k1, ssk, knit to last 3 sts, k2tog, k1; on Needle 3, k1, ssk, knit to end—4 sts dec'd.

Rnd 2: Knit.

Rep Rnds 1 and 2 until 24 (28) sts rem. Rep Rnd 1 *every* rnd until 12 sts rem. Knit the sts from Needle 1 onto the end of Needle 3—6 sts each on 2 needles.

Finishing

Cut yarn, leaving a 12" (30.5 cm) tail. Thread tail on a tapestry needle and use the Kitchener st (see Glossary, page 123) to graft sts tog.

Crocheted Edging

With RS of lace patt facing, join yarn to center back of cuff. Work 1 rnd of picot crochet (see Glossary, page 121–122, for crochet instructions) along CO edge as foll: *work 1 sc in each of next 4 CO sts, ch 3, sl st in same sc at base of ch; rep from *. Fasten off last st. For the socks shown here, the ch-3 picots are aligned with the more solid columns of the lace patt.

Weave in loose ends. Block lightly.

from the Spring 2004 issue of *Interweave Knits*

WAVING LACE SOCKS

Evelyn A. Clark

A simple lace pattern waves back and forth along the length of these socks, creating a lovely and comfortable sock that designer Evelyn Clark finds particularly soothing to knit. The socks can be started with a feminine scalloped-rib border, as shown, or with a simple knit one, purl one rib for a more tailored look. Either way, you'll love them!

FINISHED SIZE
About 7" (18 cm) foot circumference and 9" (23 cm) foot length. To fit a woman. *Note:* To make the socks larger or smaller, use needles one or two sizes larger or smaller and lengthen or shorten the foot as necessary.

YARN
Fingering-weight yarn (CYCA #1 Super Fine).
Shown here: Lorna's Laces Shepherd Sock (80% superwash wool, 20% nylon; 215 yd [196 m]/50 g): #44NS old rose, 2 skeins.

NEEDLES
Size 1 (2.25 mm): set of 5 double-pointed (dpn). Adjust needle size if necessary to obtain the correct gauge.

NOTIONS
Markers (m); tapestry needle.

GAUGE
18 stitches and 25 rounds = 2" (5 cm) in stockinette stitch worked in the round.

NOTE
The lace pattern stretches—to get an accurate length measurement, put on the sock or stretch it slightly widthwise when measuring.

Leg

Loosely CO 64 sts. Arrange sts evenly on 4 dpn (16 sts on each needle), place marker (pm), and join for working in the rnd, being careful not to twist sts. Choose scalloped edging option (shown here) or ribbed top option as foll:

Scalloped Edging Option

Work Rnds 1–14 of Scalloped Edging chart.

Ribbed Top Option

Work in k1, p1 rib for 11 rnds. *Next rnd:* *P1, k6, p1; rep from *.

Both Options

Work Rnds 1–20 of Waving Lace chart 3 times, then work Rnds 1–10 once more—piece measures about 6½" (16.5 cm) from CO.

JOE COCA

Heel

Heel Flap

Turn work and p32 heel sts onto 1 dpn. Rem 32 sts will be worked later for instep. Work 32 heel sts back and forth in rows as foll:

Row 1: (RS) *Sl 1 pwise with yarn in back (wyb), k1; rep from *.

Row 2: (WS) Sl 1 pwise with yarn in front (wyf), purl to end.

Rep these 2 rows 18 more times, then work Row 1 again—20 chain sts at each selvedge edge; heel flap measures about 2½" (6.5 cm) long.

Turn Heel

Work short-rows to shape heel as foll:

Row 1: (WS) Sl 1 pwise wyf, p16, p2tog, p1, turn.

Row 2: (RS) Sl 1 pwise wyb, k3, ssk, k1, turn.

Row 3: Sl 1 pwise wyf, p4, p2tog, p1, turn.

Row 4: Sl 1 pwise wyb, k5, ssk, k1, turn.

Cont in this manner, working 1 more st before dec each row until all of the sts have been worked—18 sts rem.

Shape Gussets

Pick up sts along selvedge edges of heel flap and rejoin for working in the rnd as foll:

Rnd 1: With Needle 1 (needle holding heel sts), pick up and knit 20 sts along selvedge edge of heel flap; divide instep sts equally between Needle 2 and Needle 3 (if they aren't already) and cont across instep sts in lace patt as established (beg with Rnd 11); with Needle 4, pick up and knit 20 sts along other selvedge edge of heel flap, then knit first 9 heel sts from Needle 1 again—90 sts total;

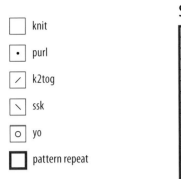

- □ knit
- • purl
- ╱ k2tog
- ╲ ssk
- ○ yo
- ▢ pattern repeat

Scalloped Edging

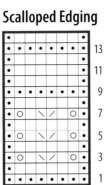

Waving Lace

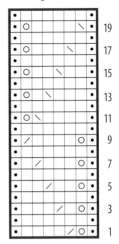

29 sts each on Needle 1 and Needle 4; 16 sts each on Needle 2 and Needle 3. Rnd begins at center of heel.

Rnd 2: On Needle 1, k9, k20 through back loops (tbl); on Needle 2 and Needle 3, cont in lace patt as established; on Needle 4, k20 tbl, k9.

Rnd 3: On Needle 1, knit to last 3 sts, k2tog, k1; on Needle 2 and Needle 3, cont in lace patt as established; on Needle 4, k1, ssk, knit to end—88 sts rem.

Rnd 4: On Needle 1, knit; on Needle 2 and Needle 3, cont in lace patt; on Needle 4, knit.

Rep Rnds 3 and 4 until 64 sts rem—16 sts on each needle.

Foot

Cont even in patt as established (work sts on Needle 2 and Needle 3 in lace patt; work sts on Needle 1 and Needle 4 in St st) until foot measures about 7½" (19 cm) from back of heel or about 1½" (3.8 cm) less

than desired total foot length, ending with an even-numbered rnd of lace patt. (To accommodate tendency of lace to stretch, try on sock or stretch it horizontally when measuring.)

Toe

Rnds 1 and 3: Knit.

Rnd 2: On Needle 1, knit to last 3 sts, k2tog, k1; on Needle 2, k1, ssk, knit to end; on Needle 3, knit to last 3 sts, k2tog, k1; on Needle 4, k1, ssk, knit to end—60 sts rem.

Rep Rnds 2 and 3 until 32 sts rem. Work Rnd 2 *only* until 12 sts rem. K3 sts from Needle 1 onto Needle 4; slip 3 sts from Needle 3 onto Needle 2—6 sts each on 2 needles.

Finishing

Cut yarn, leaving a 12" (30.5 cm) tail. Thread tail on tapestry needle and use the Kitchener st (see Glossary, page 123) to join sts tog. Weave in loose ends. Block lightly.

from the Winter 2003 issue of *Interweave Knits*

Eastern European Footlets

Priscilla Gibson-Roberts

After researching the methods Eastern European folk knitters use to work seamless intarsia in the round, Priscilla Gibson-Roberts continues to discover new techniques. These footlets are worked from toe to cuff in typical Eastern style. Unlike most seamless intarsia designs, the color work is limited to the instep. Instructions for working this type of intarsia are given on page 111.

FINISHED SIZE
About 8¼ (9½)" (21 [24] cm) foot circumference and 6¾ (8)" (17 [20.5] cm) foot length. To fit a woman (man).

YARN
Worsted-weight yarn (CYCA #4 Medium).
Shown here: Classic Elite Waterspun (100% felted merino; 138 yd [126 m]/50 g): #5046 blue spruce (MC), 2 skeins; #5026 opal basil (dark purple) and #5035 fern green, 1 skein each.
Note: This yarn has been discontinued; substitute the lightly spun worsted-weight yarn of your choice.

NEEDLES
Size 4 (3.5 mm): set of 5 double-pointed (dpn). Adjust needle size if necessary to obtain the correct gauge.

NOTIONS
Marker (m); tapestry needle.

GAUGE
14 stitches and 20 rows = 2" (5 cm) in stockinette stitch worked in the round.

STITCH GUIDE
Sssp
Slip 3 sts individually kwise, return these 3 sts to left needle, and purl them tog through their back loops.

NOTES
- Work a sample to learn the intarsia technique described on page 111 before beginning the footlets.
- While color stranding the pattern on the instep band, use short lengths of contrasting color yarns instead of balls; this allows you to pull each strand free of the others as you use it and will reduce tangling.
- If working the intarsia section while color stranding the design seems overwhelming, work the intarsia section entirely in the background color, then add the color work in duplicate stitch.

Instep

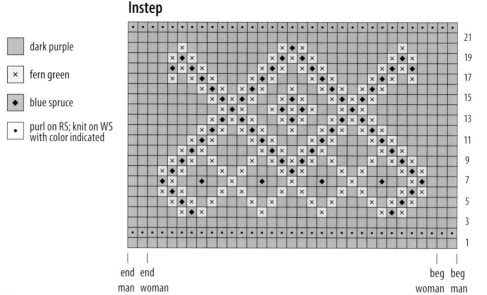

dark purple

× fern green

◆ blue spruce

· purl on RS; knit on WS with color indicated

21
19
17
15
13
11
9
7
5
3
1

| | | |
end end
man woman

beg beg
woman man

Toe

With waste yarn, MC, and using the invisible method (see Glossary, page 121), provisionally CO 29 (33) sts. Work short-rows as foll: Knit to last st (leave last st unworked), turn, backward yo (see "Heel and Toe Construction" on page 27), purl to last st (leave last st unworked), turn. *Yo as usual (from front to back), knit to 1 st before yo, turn, backward yo, purl to 1 st before yo, turn. Rep from * until there are 11 (13) sts bet yarnovers, ending with a WS row. Turn. With RS facing, yo as usual, k11 (13) to first yo, correct mount of yo (so that leading side of loop is on the front of the needle), k2tog (yo and next st), turn. Backward yo, p12 (14) to first yo on left needle, ssp (yo and next st; see Glossary, page 125). **Turn, yo as usual, knit to first yo of 2 yos, correct mount of yo loop as before, k3tog (2 yos plus the next st), turn. Backward yo, purl to first yo of 2 yos, sssp (2 yos and the next st; see Stitch Guide). Rep from ** until all sts have been worked, ending with a WS row—the last 2 turns will produce 1 yo at each end of needle. Carefully remove

waste yarn from provisional CO and place 29 (33) live sts onto 2 dpn. Knit 1 rnd, eliminating the yos by working k2tog to join first yo with first picked-up st from waste yarn, knit to last yo, ssk (see Glossary, page 122) to join last picked-up st to rem yo—58 (66) sts.

Foot

Place marker (pm) to indicate beg of rnd at side of foot. Cont even until piece measures about 4¼ (5½)" (11 [14] cm) from toe, or about 2½" (6.5 cm) less than desired length from tip of longest toe to ankle point. Working intarsia pattern as described on page 117, work Rows 1–22 of Instep chart.

Heel

The heel is worked in short-rows like the toe, beg with the underside of the heel using sts from the sole, not the sts used for the instep patt section. With MC, work to sole sts, place 29 (33) sole sts onto 1 needle for ease in working. Rem 29 (33) stitches will be worked later for instep. Work sole sts as foll: Knit

The Ultimate Intarsia Technique

When you have reached the location of your chosen pattern band, divide the stitches on four double-pointed needles (if they are not already in this arrangement) as follows: two needles to hold the instep stitches and two needles to hold the sole stitches. With main color, purl back across the sole stitches just worked (Figure 1). The main color yarn is now at the halfway point of the round. Hold the work with the main color sole yarn hanging from the left side when viewed with the instep facing you. Join the background color for instep chart at the right side of the work, the point where the row originally began, and knit across the instep stitches (Figure 2; for the project shown, this is Row 1 of the chart). Rotate the work so both yarns are now hanging from the right side when viewed with the sole facing you. Twist instep and sole yarns around each other at the side, then work back across the wrong side of the instep stitches (Figure 3: for the project shown, knit across on wrong side for Row 2 of chart). With the sole still facing you and the sole yarn already secured by having been

twisted with the instep yarn, knit across the sole stitches (Figure 4). Both yarns are again at the original beginning of the round. Rotate the work so both yarns are hanging from the right side when viewed with the instep pattern facing you. Continue as follows:

Step 1: Cross yarns at side, purl across sole stitches on wrong side.

Step 2: Knit across instep stitches on right side according to chart—1 round completed.

Step 3: Twist yarns at side, purl across instep stitches on wrong side according to chart.

Step 4: Knit across sole stitches on right side— 2 rounds completed; both working yarns are back at the original beginning of the round.

Repeat these 4 steps until instep pattern is complete.

For the project shown, the last instep row is Row 22 of chart (knit across instep stitches on the wrong side with background color). To complete the round, work across the sole stitches with main color as given in Step 4. Break off the instep color, and continue in the round with main color according to the instructions.

Figure 1

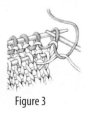

Figure 2

Figure 3

Figure 4

to last sole st (leave last st unworked), turn, backward yo, purl to last st (leave last st unworked), turn. Work as for toe from * until there are 11 (13) sts bet yarnovers, ending with a WS row. Turn. With RS facing, yo as usual, k11 (13) to first yo, correct mount of yo, k2tog (yo and next st), turn. Backward yo, p12 (14) to first yo on left needle, ssp (yo and next st). Work as for toe from ** until all sts have been worked, ending with a WS row—the last 2 turns will produce 1 yo at each end of heel needle.

Cuff

With MC, knit 1 rnd, eliminating yos as for toe—58 (66) sts. With MC, purl 1 rnd (1 garter ridge completed). Work 4 more garter ridges (knit 1 rnd, purl 1 rnd) in the foll color order: 1 green, 1 purple, 1 green, 1 MC. With MC, BO all sts.

Finishing

Weave in loose ends. Lightly steam-block.

from the Summer 2000 issue of *Interweave Knits*

Up-Down Spiral Sox

Sandy Cushman

These comfortable roll-top socks are an adventure in unusual construction: they can be knitted from the toe up or the cuff down, and they feature an "afterthought heel" worked from held stitches after the rest of the sock is completed. To make the mirrored spiral, the color pattern is worked in the opposite direction on the second sock.

FINISHED SIZE

About 7½ (8)" (19 [20.5] cm) foot circumference and about 9¼ (10)" (23.5 [25.5] cm) foot length. To fit a woman (man).

YARN

Sportweight yarn (CYCA #2 Fine).

Shown here: Plymouth Cleckheaton Country 8-Ply (100% washable wool; 106 yd [97 m]/50 g): #18 red (MC), 2 balls, #9215 grayish green, 1 ball. Plymouth Cleckheaton Tapestry (100% washable wool; 109 yd [100 m]/50 g): #5 multicolored (CC), 1 ball. *Note:* The contrast-color yarn has been discontinued; substitute the sportweight washable wool of your choice.

NEEDLES

Size 5 (3.75 mm): set of 5 double-pointed (dpn). Adjust needle size if necessary to obtain the correct gauge.

NOTIONS

Small amount of contrasting waste yarn; markers (m); tapestry needle.

GAUGE

12 stitches and 14 rows = 2" (5 cm) in slip-stitch pattern, unblocked; 11 stitches = 2" (5 cm), blocked.

STITCH GUIDE

Slip-Stitch Pattern (multiple of 4 sts)

Rnds 1 and 2: With CC, *k3, sl 1; rep from *.

Rnds 3 and 4: With MC, sl 1, *k3, sl 1; rep from *, end k3.

Rnds 5 and 6: With CC, k1, sl 1, *k3, sl 1; rep from *, end k2.

Rnds 7 and 8: With MC, k2, sl 1, *k3, sl 1; rep from *, end k1.

Repeat Rnds 1–8 for a right-leaning pattern.

Work the opposite direction (Rnds 8–1) for a left-leaning pattern.

NOTES

- Rounds begin at the inside of the foot; hence, the instep stitches are worked first for the right sock and the sole stitches are worked first for the left sock to place "seam" (color changes) at inside of leg, where they are least noticeable.
- At color changes, always bring the new yarn *under* the old to prevent holes.

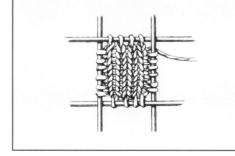
Toe-Up Version
Right Sock

Toe

With red, CO 4 sts. Beg with a knit row, work these 4 sts in St st for 9 rows. With RS facing, use 3 other dpn to pick up and knit 6 sts along one side edge, 4 sts across CO edge, and 6 sts along other side edge (see box above), then knit the first 2 sts from the original 4—20 sts total. Place marker (pm) and join, arranging sts so that there are 5 sts on each of 4 dpn and placing a second marker between the 10th and 11th sts.

Shape Toe

Beg with red and alternating 2 rnds red with 2 rnds green, inc as foll:

Rnds 1, 3, 5, 7, and 9: Knit.

Rnds 2, 4, 6, 8, and 10: K1, M1 (see Glossary, page 124), knit to 1 st before m, M1, k2, M1, knit to 1 st before m, M1, k1—4 sts inc'd each rnd; 40 sts after Rnd 10.

Rnd 11: Knit.

Size small only:

Rnd 12: K1, M1, knit to 1 st before m, M1, knit to end—42 sts.

Rnd 13: Knit.

Rnd 14: Knit to m, k1, M1, knit to 1 st before m, M1, k1—44 sts.

Size large only:

Rnd 12: K1, M1, knit to 1 st before m, M1, k2, M1, knit to 1 st before m, M1, k1—44 sts.

Rnd 13: Knit.

Rnd 14: K1, M1, knit to 1 st before m, M1, knit to end—46 sts.

Rnd 15: Knit.

Rnd 16: K1, M1, knit to 1 st before m, M1, knit to end—48 sts.

Foot

Knit 0 (2) rnds red. Break off green. Join multicolored yarn and work Rnds 1–8 of slip-stitch patt (see Stitch Guide) until piece measures about 7 (7½)" (18 [19] cm) from beg, or about 2¼ (2½)" (5.5 [6.5] cm) less than desired total foot length (including heel), ending with an even-numbered rnd.

Mark Heel Opening

Cont in patt across first 22 (24) sts for instep, drop main yarn. With contrasting waste yarn, k22 (24) sts for heel, then drop contrasting yarn and work these 22 (24) sts again with main yarn. Knit to end of rnd. *Note:* Do not work slip-st patt on the 22 (24) heel sts for 2 rnds. Resume patt on all sts on the next odd-numbered rnd of patt.

Leg

Cont in patt until piece measures about
2¼" (5.5 cm) less than desired total length
to top.

Border

[Knit 2 rnds red, knit 2 rnds green] 3 times—
6 stripes. With red, knit 5 rnds. BO all sts
loosely.

Heel

Place dpn through the 22 (24) sts on each
side of the waste yarn, then carefully remove
waste yarn as illustrated below. Arrange sts
so that there are 11 (12) leg sts on each of
2 dpn and 11 (12) foot sts on each of 2 other
dpn—44 (48) sts total. With red and beg at
the gap between the leg and foot sts, pick
up and knit 2 sts in gap, k22 (24), pick up
and knit 4 sts in the gap on the other side,
placing m between the 2nd and 3rd picked-
up st, k22 (24), then pick up and knit 2 sts in
the first gap—52 (56) sts total. Place m and
join. K1, ssk, knit to 3 sts from next m, k2tog,
k1; rep from *—4 sts dec'd. Alternating
2 rnds green with 2 rnds red, dec in this
manner every other rnd 7 times total—24
(28) sts rem. Then dec *every* rnd until 12 sts
rem. Knit 1 rnd.

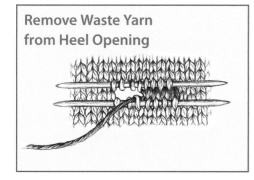

**Remove Waste Yarn
from Heel Opening**

Finishing

With yarn threaded on a tapestry needle,
use the Kitchener st (see Glossary, page 123)
to graft rem sts tog. Weave in loose ends.
Block lightly.

Toe-Up Version
Left Sock

Work as for right sock, but work slip-stitch
patt in the opposite direction (Rnds 8–1)
and mark the heel opening on the *first*
22 (24) sts of the rnd.

Leg-Down Version
Right Sock

Leg

With red, loosely CO 44 (48) sts. Arrange sts evenly on 4 dpn, place marker (pm), and join for working in the rnd, being careful not to twist sts.

Border

Knit 5 rnds. [Knit 2 rnds green, knit 2 rnds red] 3 times. Beg with Rnd 1, work slip-stitch patt (see Stitch Guide) until piece measures 5½ (6)" (14 [15] cm) from beg, or desired length to ankle bone, ending with an even-numbered rnd.

Mark Heel Opening

Cont in patt across first 22 (24) sts for instep, drop main yarn. With contrasting waste yarn k22 (24) sts for heel, then drop contrasting yarn and work these 22 (24) sts again with main yarn. Knit to end of rnd. *Note:* Do not work slip-st patt on the 22 (24) heel sts for 2 rnds. Resume patt on all sts on the next odd-numbered row of chart.

Foot

Cont in patt until piece measures about 2 (2½)" (5 [6.5] cm) less than desired total foot length.

Toe

Alternating 2 rnds red with 2 rnds green, dec as foll:

Rnds 1, 3, 5, 7, 9, and 11: Knit.

Rnds 2, 4, 6, 8, 10, and 12: K1, ssk, knit to m, k2tog, k2, ssk, knit to m, k2tog, k1— 4 sts dec'd each rnd; 20 (24) sts rem after Rnd 12.

Size small only:

Rnds 13 and 14: Knit, dec 4 sts as before— 12 sts rem after Rnd 14.

Rnd 15: Knit.

Size large only:

Rnd 13: Knit.

Rnds 14, 15, and 16: Knit, dec 4 sts as before—12 sts rem after Rnd 16.

Rnd 17: Knit.

Both sizes:

Break yarn, leaving a long tail. With tail threaded on a tapestry needle, use the Kitchener st (see Glossary, page 123) to graft sts tog.

Heel

Work as for toe-up version.

Leg-Down Version
Left Sock

Work as for right sock, but work slip-stitch patt in the opposite direction (Rnds 8–1) and mark the heel opening on the first 22 (24) sts of the rnd.

Finishing

Weave in loose ends. Block lightly.

CONTRIBUTORS

Erica Alexander learned to knit more than twenty years ago but waited ten years to knit her first sock. Since then, she's "always got a pair on the needles" and boasts that she hasn't worn a store-bought sock for years.

Jennifer L. Appleby designs knitwear with a view of British Columbia's "wilderness" outside her windows. Her days are kept busy running her yarn shop, adding to her Woollen Earth leaflet collection (which sells in shops throughout North America), and designing for magazines and books. Visit her website at www.thewoollenearth.com.

Ann Budd loves to knit and especially loves to knit socks. She is a book editor for Interweave Press and author of the *Knitter's Handy Book* series.

Nancy Bush has a passion for traditional hand-knitting, which has encouraged her passion for knitting socks. Her designs and articles have appeared in *Interweave Knits*, *Vogue Knitting*, *Knitter's*, and *PieceWork*. She owns The Wooly West, a mail-order and online yarn source. She is the author of *Folk Socks*, *Folk Knitting in Estonia*, *Knitting on the Road*, and *Knitting Vintage Socks*, all published by Interweave Press.

Evelyn A. Clark lives in Seattle, Washington, where she enjoys finding new ways to make holes in her knitting.

Sandy Cushman studied painting in textiles at the Rhode Island School of Design. She currently paints and dyes her own yarns and hand prints her own fabrics for garments and home design. Depending on the season, she can be found biking or skiing near her home in Durango, Colorado.

Priscilla Gibson-Roberts loves to make socks and learn about traditional knitting. In addition to contributing patterns to *Interweave Knits*, her work includes the titles *Knitting in the Old Way*, *Spinning in the Old Way*, and two books of sock patterns.

Wayne Pfeffer still knits, after taking it up in 1956 a as sophomore in college. He lives outside Centralia, Missouri, on the piece of wooded land he bought forty years ago. He also spins some of his own yarn and occasionally weaves.

Mona Schmidt knits socks for family members and friends in Montréal, Quebec, and is the Associate Creative Director of JCA Inc.

Mary Snyder's formal training is in designing rocket and satellite communication systems, but her passions are knitting, spinning, and making fine silver tools and accessories for knitters and spinners. Visit her website at www.MarySnyderDesigns.com.

Jaya Srikrishnan has been knitting for most of her life. She is an accomplished designer and teacher who loves to share her expertise and enthusiasm with other knitters. Her designs have been published in *Cast On*, *Interweave Knits*, and *INKnitters*, as well as various books, and she teaches regularly in and around her hometown of Wappingers Falls, New York.

Candace Eisner Strick is an internationally known knitwear designer, author, and teacher. Her new line of yarn, Merging Colors, made its debut in 2006, offering knitters a unique new experience of colorful knitting. Candace loves traditional Austrian knitting designs and uses them whenever her brain needs exercising.

Anne Woodbury is the ever-proud mother of two sons, one in high school and one in college. She spends her days volunteering, working in her organic vegetable garden, and knitting (of course). She loves living in the suburbs of Portland, Oregon.

GLOSSARY

ABBREVIATIONS

beg	begin(s); beginning	**rev St st**	reverse stockinette stitch
BO	bind off	**rnd(s)**	round(s)
CC	contrast color	**RS**	right side
ch	crochet chain	**sc**	single crochet
cm	centimeter(s)	**sl**	slip
cn	cable needle	**sl st**	slip st (slip 1 st pwise unless
CO	cast on		otherwise indicated)
dec(s)	decrease(s); decreasing	**ssk**	slip, slip, knit (decrease)
dpn	double-pointed needles	**ssp**	slip, slip, purl (decrease)
g	gram(s)	**sssp**	slip, slip, slip, purl (double
inc(s)	increase(s); increasing		decrease)
k	knit	**st(s)**	stitch(es)
k1f&b	knit into the front and back of	**St st**	stockinette stitch
	same st	**tbl**	through back loop
kwise	knitwise; as if to knit	**tog**	together
m	marker(s)	**WS**	wrong side
MC	main color	**wyb**	with yarn in back
mm	millimeter(s)	**wyf**	with yarn in front
M1	make one (increase)	**yd**	yard(s)
p	purl	**yo**	yarnover
p1f&b	purl into front and back of	*****	repeat starting point
	same st	******	repeat all instructions between
patt(s)	pattern(s)		asterisks
psso	pass slipped st over	**( )**	alternate measurements and/
pwise	purlwise; as if to purl		or instructions
rem	remain(s); remaining	**[ ]**	instructions worked as a group a
rep	repeat(s)		specified number of times.

CAST-ONS

1 x 1 Rib Cast-On

Leaving a long tail (about ½" [1.3 cm] for each stitch to be cast on), make a slipknot and place on right needle. The slipknot counts as the first stitch. Place thumb and index finger of your left hand between the yarn ends so that working yarn is around your index finger and tail end is around your thumb, then secure the yarn ends with your other fingers. Hold your palm upwards, making a V of yarn. There will be four strands of yarn: 1, 2, 3, and 4 (Figure 1). *Bring the needle under strand 1, from front to back, then bring it over the top of strand 3 (Figure 2) and down through the loop around your thumb (Figure 3). Drop the loop off your thumb and, placing your thumb back in the V configuration, tighten up the resulting stitch on the needle. Then bring the needle under strand 4, from back to front, then over the top of strand 2 (Figure 4) and back through the loop around your index finger. Drop the loop off your index finger (Figure 5) and, placing your index finger back in the V configuration, tighten up the resulting stitch on the needle. There will now be 2 more stitches on the needle. Repeat from * for the desired number of stitches.

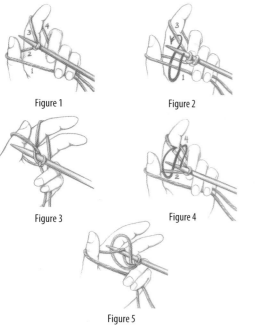

Figure 1 Figure 2

Figure 3 Figure 4

Figure 5

Knitted Cast-On

Make a slipknot of working yarn and place on the left needle if there are no stitches already there. *Use the right needle to knit the first stitch (or slipknot) on left needle (Figure 1) and place new loop onto left needle to form a new stitch (Figure 2). Repeat from * for the desired number of stitches, always knitting into the last stitch made.

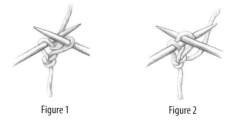

Figure 1 Figure 2

Long-Tail (Continental) Cast-On

Leaving a long tail (about ½" [1.3 cm] for each stitch to be cast on), make a slipknot and place on right needle. Place thumb and index finger of your left hand between the yarn ends so that working yarn is around your index finger and tail end is around your thumb and secure the yarn ends with your other fingers. Hold your palm upwards, making a V of yarn (Figure 1). *Bring needle up through loop on thumb (Figure 2), catch first strand around index finger, and go back down through loop on thumb (Figure 3). Drop loop off thumb and, placing thumb back in V configuration, tighten resulting stitch on needle (Figure 4). Repeat from * for the desired number of stitches.

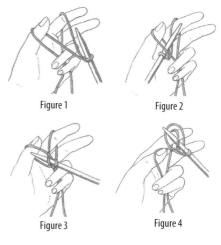

Figure 1 Figure 2

Figure 3 Figure 4

Old Norwegian Cast-On

Leaving a long tail (about ½" [1.3 cm] for each stitch to be cast on), make a slipknot and place on right needle. Place thumb and index finger between yarn ends so that the working yarn is around your index finger and the tail end is around your thumb. Secure the ends with your other fingers and hold your palm upward, making a V of yarn (Figure 1). *Bring needle in front of thumb, under both yarns around thumb, down into center of thumb loop, back forward, and over top of yarn around index finger (Figure 2), catch this yarn and bring needle back down through thumb loop (Figure 3), turning thumb slightly to make room for needle to pass through. Drop loop off thumb (Figure 4) and place thumb back in V configuration while tightening up resulting stitch on needle. Repeat from * for the desired number of stitches.

Figure 1

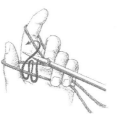

Figure 2

Figure 3

Figure 4

Provisional (Invisible) Cast-On

Make a loose slipknot of working yarn and place it on the right needle. Hold a length of waste yarn next to the slipknot and around your left thumb; hold working yarn over your left index finger. *Bring right needle forward under waste yarn, over working yarn, grab a loop of working yarn (Figure 1), then bring needle to the front over both yarns and grab a second loop (Figure 2). Repeat from * for the desired number of stitches. When you're ready to work in the opposite direction, place the exposed loops on a knitting needle as you pull out the waste yarn.

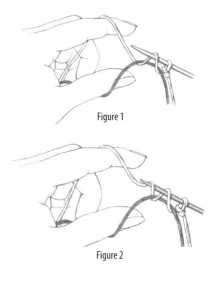

Figure 1

Figure 2

CROCHET

Crochet Chain (ch)

Make a slipknot and place it on crochet hook. *Yarn over hook and draw through loop on hook. Repeat from * for the desired number of stitches. To fasten off, cut yarn and draw end through last loop formed.

Single Crochet (sc)

*Insert hook into the second chain from the hook, yarn over hook and draw through a loop, yarn over hook (Figure 1), and draw it through both loops on hook (Figure 2). Repeat from * for the desired number of stitches. At the end of the row, chain 2 stitches and turn the work around. Begin the next row by inserting the hook into the second stitch from hook.

Figure 1

Figure 2

Slip Stitch Crochet (sl st)

*Insert hook into stitch, yarn over hook and draw a loop through both the stitch and loop already on hook. Repeat from * for the desired number of stitches.

DECREASES

K2tog

Knit 2 stitches together as if they were a single stitch.

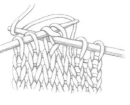

P2tog

Purl 2 stitches together as if they were a single stitch.

Ssk

Slip 2 stitches individually knitwise (Figure 1), insert left needle tip into the front of these 2 slipped stitches, and use the right needle to knit them together through their back loops (Figure 2).

Figure 1

Figure 2

Ssp

Holding yarn in front, slip 2 stitches individually knitwise (Figure 1), then slip these 2 stitches back onto left needle (they will appear twisted) and purl them together through their back loops (Figure 2).

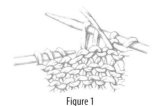

Figure 1

Figure 2

GRAFTING

Kitchener Stitch

Arrange stitches on 2 needles so that there is the same number of stitches on each needle. Hold the needles parallel to each other with right sides of the knitting facing up. Allowing about ½" (1.3 cm) per stitch to be grafted, thread matching yarn on a tapestry needle. Work from right to left as follows:

Step 1. Bring tapestry needle through the first stitch on the front needle as if to purl and leave the stitch on the needle (Figure 1).

Step 2. Bring tapestry needle through the first stitch on the back needle as if to knit and leave that stitch on the needle (Figure 2).

Step 3. Bring tapestry needle through the first front stitch as if to knit and slip this stitch off the needle, then bring tapestry needle through the next front stitch as if to purl and leave this stitch on the needle (Figure 3).

Step 4. Bring tapestry needle through the first back stitch as if to purl and slip this stitch off the needle, then bring tapestry needle through the next back stitch as if to knit and leave this stitch on the needle (Figure 4).

Repeat Steps 3 and 4 until no stitches remain on the needles, adjusting the tension to match the rest of the knitting as you go.

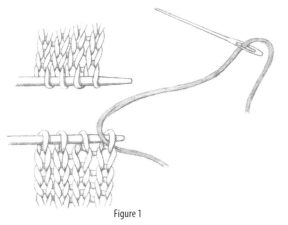

Figure 1

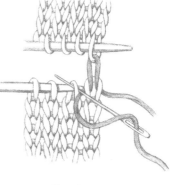

Figure 3

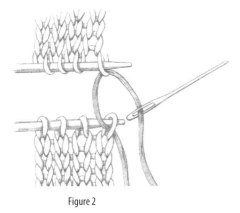

Figure 2

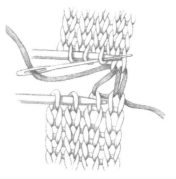

Figure 4

I-CORD

Using 2 double-pointed needles, cast on the desired number of stitches (usually 3 to 4). *Without turning the needle, slide stitches to other end of needle, pull the yarn around the back, and knit the stitches as usual. Repeat from * for desired length.

INCREASES

K1f&b

Knit into a stitch but leave it on the left needle (Figure 1), then knit through the back loop of the same stitch (Figure 2) and slip the original stitch off the needle.

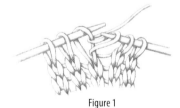

Figure 1

Figure 2

Make One (M1)

With left needle tip, lift the strand between last knitted stitch and first stitch on left needle from front to back (Figure 1), then knit the lifted loop through the back (Figure 2).

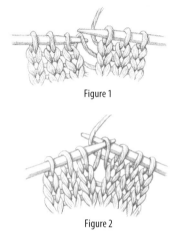

Figure 1

Figure 2

Make One Purlwise (M1pwise)

With left needle tip, lift strand between needles, from back to front (Figure 1). Purl lifted loop (Figure 2).

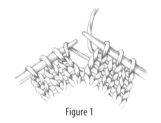

Figure 1

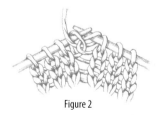

Figure 2

Yarnover (yo)

Wrap the working yarn around the needle from front to back, then bring yarn into position to work the next stitch (leave it in back if a knit stitch follows; bring it under the needle to the front if a purl stitch follows).

Yarnover backwards (backward yo)

Bring the yarn to the back under the needle, then over the top to the front so that the leading leg of the loop is at the back of the needle.

PICK UP AND PURL

With wrong side facing and working from right to left while holding yarn in front, insert tip of needle from back to front under the selvedge stitch (Figure 1), wrap yarn around needle, and pull it through to form a stitch on the needle (Figure 2).

 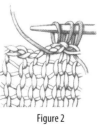

Figure 1   Figure 2

PICK UP AND KNIT

With right side facing and working from right to left, insert tip of needle under the front half (Figure 1) or both halves (Figure 2) of stitch along selvedge edge, wrap yarn around needle, and pull it through to form a stitch on the needle. For a tighter join, pick up the stitches and knit them through the back loop (Figure 3).

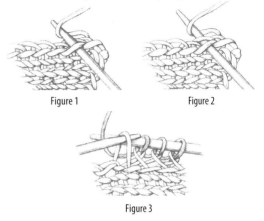

Figure 1   Figure 2

Figure 3

SHORT-ROWS

Work to turning point, slip next stitch purlwise to right needle, then bring the yarn to the front (Figure 1). Slip the same stitch back to the left needle (Figure 2), turn the work around and bring the yarn in position for the next stitch, wrapping the slipped stitch with working yarn as you do so. When you come to a wrapped stitch on a subsequent row, hide the wrap by working it together with the wrapped stitch as follows: Insert right needle tip under the wrap (from the front if wrapped stitch is a knit stitch; from the back if wrapped stitch is a purl stitch), then into the stitch on the needle, and work the stitch and its wrap together as a single stitch.

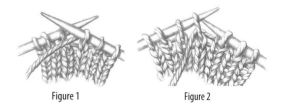

Figure 1   Figure 2

Supplies

Artemis Exquisite Embellishments
(888) 233-5187
www.artimisinc.com
Hannah Silk Ribbon

Brown Sheep Company
100662 County Rd. 16
Mitchell, NE 69357
(308) 635-2198
www.brownsheep.com
*Lamb's Pride Superwash Worsted
(CYCA #4 Medium)
Nature Spun Sport (CYCA #2 Fine)
Wildfoote (CYCA #1 Super Fine)*

Cascade Yarns
PO Box 58168
1224 Andover Park East
Tukwila, WA 98188
(206) 574-0440
www.cascadeyarns.com
Fixation (CYCA #2 Fine)

Cherry Tree Hill
100 Cherry Tree Hill Ln.
Barton, VT 05822
www.cherryyarn.com
Supersock Solids (CYCA #1 Fine)

Classic Elite Yarns
300 Jackson St.
Lowell, MA 01852
www.classiceliteyarns.com
Waterspun (CYCA #4 Medium)

Dale of Norway
N16 W23390 Stone Ridge Dr., Ste. A
Waukesha, WI 53188
www.dale.no
*Heilo (CYCA #2 Fine)
Tiur (CYCA #2 Fine)*

Knit One Crochet Too
7 Commons Ave., Ste. 2
Windham, ME 04062
www.knitonecrochettoo.com
Richesse et Soie (CYCA #1 Super Fine)

Koigu Wool Designs
RR# 1
Williamsford, ON
Canada N0H 2V0
(519) 794-3066, (888) 765-WOOL
www.koigu.com
*Koigu Premium Merino
(CYCA #1 Super Fine)*

Lana Grossa

Distributed in the United States and Canada
by Unicorn Books & Crafts Inc.
1338 Ross St.
Petaluma, CA 94954
(707) 762-3362; (800) 289-9276
www.lanagrossa.com
  Meilenweit Cotton (CYCA #1 Super Fine)

Lorna's Laces Yarns

4229 N. Honore St.
Chicago, IL 60613
www.lornaslaces.net
  Shepherd Sock (CYCA #1 Super Fine)

Louet Sales

808 Commerce Park Dr.
Odgensburg, NY 13669
(613) 925-4502; (800) 897-6444
www.louet.com
  Gems Pearl (CYCA #1 Super Fine)
  Gems Opal (CYCA #2 Fine)
  MerLin Tristan (CYCA #2 Fine)

Patons/Spinrite

320 Livingstone Ave., South
Listowel, ON
Canada N4W 3H3
www.patonsyarn.com
  Kroy Socks (CYCA #1 Super Fine)
  Rustic Wool (CYCA #4 Medium)

Plymouth Yarn Company

PO Box 28
Bristol, PA 19007
(215) 788-0459
www.plymouthyarn.com
  Cleckeheaton Tapestry (CYCA #2 Fine)
  Cleckheaton Country 8-Ply
    (CYCA #4 Medium)

Skacel Collections

PO Box 88110
Seattle, WA 98138
www.skacelknitting.com
  Scholler Esslinger Fortissima Colori
    (CYCA #1 Super Fine)
  Scholler-Stahl Zimba Top
    (CYCA #1 Super Fine)
  Scholler-Stahl Wolle Ole
    (CYCA #2 Fine)
  Zitron Trekking Tweed XXL
    (CYCA #1 Super Fine)

Vourelman

Available in the United States from
Schoolhouse Press
6899 Cary Bluff
Pittsville, WI 54466
www.schoolhousepress.com
  and
Wooly West
PO Box 58306
Salt Lake City, UT 84158
www.woolywest.com
    Satakieli (CYCA #1 Super Fine)

INDEX